SELECTING THE SITE

Patios have never been more popular than they are today, as we become more and more aware of the value of precious living space out of doors. Somewhere to sit, to play, to entertain out in the open extends the living area of your house and adds another dimension to leisure life, especially if you are able to cook outside, too, on occasions.

Opposite page Basic patio layout at the rear of the house, with mixed paving and including a mini-pool. At left the pergola and overhead beams, offering support for climbing plants, provide partial shade for the table and bench seating, built-in barbecue and storage units.

A patio is an expensive item to construct, so it's important to get the design and the planning right. But before you get to the actual planning stage, there are a few questions to ask yourself about the site. Traditionally we think of the patio as an area alongside the house, but this need not necessarily be so: it all depends on how you are going to use it. Is it to be an outdoor room? It could be that you are overlooked, or that the garden is in shade all the time, or that the street is so noisy that you are not likely to want to stay outdoors for long. In this case, you may decide to use your patio mainly as an area filled with attractive plants that can be viewed from the window. A paved area is a very good way of showing off a series of tubs, boxes and baskets of flowers that can be switched around with the seasons and replenished with bedding plants.

Many people have to use their patio primarily as a service area. For instance, you may have to store dustbins in it, or hang out the washing across it, or use at least part of the total space to keep a bicycle, scooter, or push-chair under cover. In such cases you may want to arrange for trellises or other types of screens to hide all the impedimenta and still leave you room for a deckchair or for sunbathing. So the patio may need to be larger than you might otherwise have envisaged. A patio that is to be a young children's playground, on the other hand, does not necessarily need the sun; but it should have a non-slip surface and be near enough to the kitchen door for you to be able to keep an eye on things.

Work out which way your plot faces in relation to the sun's position at various times of the day and how it might affect your use of a patio. You may find, for instance, when you come to chart the sunshine, that the spot where you are planning to sunbathe in the afternoon, in a small backyard or garden, will be in the shade at that time of day; in which case you will have to think again. Remember that in summer the sun climbs higher in the sky and you get longer hours of heat and light. The ideal patio faces south or west for the maximum warmth and sunshine. If it is sunbathing at all costs that you want from your patio you may find you need to

site it away from the house, perhaps even at the far end of your garden. This might have the bonus of giving you more peace and quiet, distanced from the hurly-burly of the house.

Screening off the area from the eyes of the neighbours and ensuring privacy plays its part in the planning of most patios; but it should be done in such a way that it does not put the garden or the patio itself into shade or make it feel cramped. This can often be done by using a see-through structure such as trellis or pierced-screen concrete blocks, rather than a solid wall. But remember that the higher the fence, the less sunshine it will let in. In cramped city conditions a 'ceiling' of laths or planks suspended on their edges, with creepers growing over and between them, can block out the upstairs neighbours' view of you and give you the feeling that you are in your own outdoor dining room. If you want to, you can add clear, corrugated PVC sheeting on top, which will shut out the worst of the weather and act as a greenhouse over the climbers beneath; but it will be very noisy when it rains hard. Any such roofing, incidentally, should have a slight slope so that the rain runs off it. You can also use the space under the planks to suspend plant pots and hanging baskets.

Right An archway, well clothed with climbers, creates a sense of anticipation by concealing what lies beyond in this Leeds council-house garden.

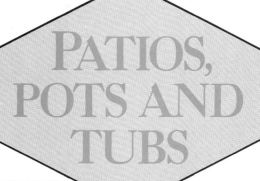

PATIOS, POTS AND TUBS

HAZEL EVANS

CONTENTS

First published in 1986 by
Octopus Books Limited,
59 Grosvenor Street, London W1

© 1986 Hennerwood Publications Limited
ISBN 0 86273 293 X
Printed and bound in Great Britain
by Jarrold and Sons Limited, Norwich

INTRODUCTION

Fashions come and go with as much speed in the gardening world as they do in the world of haute couture – but one creation looks set for a long and popular reign, and that's the patio.

Estate agents love the word: to read their eloquent house descriptions you'd think that every terrace property was blessed with a patio, when usually a gloomy backyard is what's on offer. But with ingenuity that backyard can easily become a patio at very little expense.

Hazel Evans gardens in the centre of London and knows just what it takes to transform an unimpressive patch of earth or concrete into that romantic-sounding 'green oasis'.

The biggest attraction a patio offers is relaxation among the flowers; but it's not just idleness that accounts for a rash of patios countrywide, it's the fact that the outdoor room bridges the gap most comfortably between house and garden – however grand or modest the two may be.

Don't feel obliged to curtail your ambitions to fit the size of your plot: a small pool with a fountain illuminated at night can thrill as much as the giant cascades at Chatsworth because the effect is unexpected.

But all this creativity takes time and energy. Hazel Evans doesn't lead you up the garden path: she explains just what's needed when it comes to laying paving or gravel, and which plants are especially suited to being grown in containers of infinite variety. She'll prevent you from turning your sitting-out area into a multi-coloured chess-board by showing you more surfaces than you knew existed – from slabs and bricks to cobbles and gravel and decking.

Children will probably use the patio even more than you will, and there are ideas here to help you live in harmony!

In our present house, the patio outside the back door was the first thing we built. There are fences covered with flowering and foliage climbers, beds packed with plants that flower and fruit at different seasons, and masses of pots and tubs with bulbs for winter, rhododendrons for spring, bedding plants for summer and foliage plants for autumn. We live on that patch of crazy paving whenever the weather is remotely favourable.

With any luck this book will convert you to the outdoor life – even if you're a confirmed insider. There's nothing to compare with putting your feet up on a warm day, surrounded by flowers and leaves and butterflies and bees, even if the odd wasp does land in your drink, and the occasional spider sends you scuttling for cover.

PLANNING THE PATIO

No matter how small your patio is going to be, it pays to make a plan. But first of all, if you are doing anything drastic, you need to check that you are not contravening local bye-laws or a landlord's agreement. It is far better to find out beforehand than to have to put things right afterwards – expensively. Remember that many trees now have preservation orders on them, especially in towns; this is a point that needs checking too. It is useful at this stage to find out what type of soil you have – acid, alkaline (limy), or neutral. And find out whether it is sticky clay or a lightweight sand that will let the moisture drain through. If you are gardening solely in containers then you can choose your own compost to suit yourself and the plants you wish to select. Otherwise, a chat with the neighbours or the use of a soil-testing kit will give you a guide-line when it comes to choosing plants. If you have no-one else to turn to, your local town parks department may be of help.

DESIGN

Note any existing features that are there and plan to make the most of them. Even a dead woody shrub or tree may be useful as a host to climbing plants or to suspend hanging baskets from. Other factors must also be taken into consideration. Are you overlooked by a high-rise building, for instance, which shuts out a lot of light? Is yours a site that gets more than its fair share of wind? Decide, too, whether you want to block out your surroundings or make a feature of them. Often an item like a church spire or a magnificent tree across the road can make a punctuation point outside your garden that you want to keep in view, while an ugly factory or lines of neighbours' washing will need screening from sight.

Fences and walls are a precious bonus to the confined gardener: they are the features where you can get some of your most spectacular effects with climbers planted in half baskets; you can even exploit them to deceive the eye by painting murals on them or by using mirrors. Think carefully about the patio 'floor'. What is it going to be used for? Heavy-duty traffic may dictate the use of concrete or natural stone paving; but they can be jazzed up by growing little crevice plants between them – a point to bear in mind when laying the slabs. Remember, though, that the use of paving under a deciduous tree or a bush that bears lots of berries may mean that you will have a great deal of sweeping up to do when autumn comes if it is not to look unsightly, and it may pay you to have grass or a grass substitute instead.

If a patch of lawn is out of the question, but you yearn for one, then you can have a miniature patch of green chamomile or some other creeping plant that makes a good grass substitute simply by leaving out one or two of the paving stones at random and planting up the spaces.

Even the smallest patio needs a focal point of

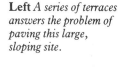

some sort – something that focuses your attention when you view it. A small statue, if it is carefully chosen, can lead the eye to the end of a small courtyard. A sundial makes a good centre point to a paved garden. A small pool looks good, especially if it is raised above ground level for dramatic effect. Water makes an ever changing centre of interest, especially in confined surroundings.

Patio lighting is another item to be taken into consideration at this stage, since it is much easier to instal right at the beginning, when wiring can be hidden, than having to disguise trailing flexes later on. If you are planning a barbecue, remember that you will need to provide suitable lighting around it for evening cook-outs. A permanent fixture above head height is best.

While you are still at the planning stage it is a good idea to develop an overall theme for your patio. It could be a particular colour scheme: small patio areas look best with one, rather than a liquorice-allsorts mix of every conceivable colour. Or it could be a particular 'look'. If you wanted to make your plot look like a Mediterranean-style patio, for instance, you could plan for some large terracotta pots, and make up a shopping list of plants like the yucca, and the Chusan palm (*Trachycarpus fortunei*) or New Zealand flax (*Phormium tenax*) to give a spicy, sub-tropical look. A country-garden patio can easily be achieved by heavy interplanting among the paving slabs and with old-fashioned flowers like foxgloves (*Digitalis*) and hollyhocks (*Althaea*) against the wall.

Left *A series of terraces answers the problem of paving this large, sloping site.*

Below *Large sliding garden doors allow this living room and patio to become fully integrated on warm summer days.*

MAKING YOUR PLAN

Drawing up a plan of your patio gives you a chance to make your mistakes on paper rather than more expensively on the site. The easiest way to do this is to make a large-scale plan of your plot on graph paper. Using the squares to count, rather than measuring each time, saves a great deal of effort. And you can sketch in the approximate size of fully grown specimen plants to see how they will look. Better still, cut them out of pieces of paper and move them around on your plan to find the best position for them. If you are proposing to include deckchairs, cushions, or a table and chairs, cut out scale outlines of the furniture separately and move them around on your plan to see if they will fit. You will need to attend to such details as making sure that it is actually possible to push a chair back from the table when you want to stand up, especially if you are building a terrace in a confined space or planning to cram a number of containers onto it. For a really comfortable sitting-out area that will take a table seating four people, you need a width of at least 2.5m (8¼ft) and as much length as is available.

As a general rule, keep the centre of the patio open, otherwise the immediate outlook from the house will seem cluttered. Bear in mind, too, if you are planning raised flowerbeds or putting plants against a house wall where there has never been a bed before, that you must not go above the damp-course line or you may be plagued with moisture problems on the inside of the house. You will find the damp-course if you look for a layer of tarred felt or other material inserted between courses of bricks near the ground on newer houses or, on older properties, such features as a series of holes bored in the wall. Where no damp course is evident, follow the general guide that the soil level should be a good 150mm (6in) below the floor level inside the house. If you do come up against the problem of damp, you must move the flower-bed away from the wall, put your plants in free-standing containers, or instal some sort of permanent waterproof sheeting between the soil and the brickwork. Another simple idea is to use growing bags. You can disguise these useful but unattractive plastic containers in various ways – for instance, with a row of pot-grown herbs.

If, when you have drawn up your plan and put it on paper, you are still a little doubtful how the

The patio can be a place of restful relaxation. Here, for instance, a small paved area is separated from the noise and bustle of the house by a pierced-screen-block wall and the lawn beyond.

Tiny town gardens can provide a colourful display with space-saving 'vertical' plantings, narrow borders and small container plants.

overall plan or some of its main features will look in reality, it's a good idea to take photographs of the site from several angles. You can then sketch the major features you are proposing, like specimen trees, raised beds, a barbecue, or walls and screens, on to the photos. This will help you to see what your plan will look like in a third dimension. Now try your plan out on the actual site, using buckets as containers and pieces of wood and any other props you please. You may find that what seemed to work on paper does not quite work out in practice. Perhaps the door or window will not open fully, for instance, because something is in the way. Mark out paved areas, flower beds, and so on with a string and wooden pegs. Keep the string above ground level to give a more realistic feel of that third dimension, height: a planned area picked out in chalk on the ground may seem to work out nicely – but may become obtrusive when you see it in terms of growing plants. If your plot slopes, do not be in too much of a hurry to level it up. Think carefully first: it might be better to turn it into a series of terraces. Or the slope could be exploited by installing a feature with an attractive trickle of water down to a pool.

A small, steep-sloping site has been cleverly converted here into intimate upper and lower terraces, whose circular form is echoed in the shape of the pool and flights of steps.

MATERIALS

The materials for your patio are likely to be the largest single expenditure you will make on your garden, so it is as well to make the right choice. There is a wide range of surfaces available now, each with its own advantages and disadvantages. You need to list your own particular requirements in order of importance, then choose the material that suits you best.

Used creatively, a hard surface outside can enhance the look of your house. But you must at all costs avoid producing a desolate, hard-ground cover reminiscent of a shopping precinct. So think, in general, about breaking up the hard-surface layout into fairly small areas, varying the surfacing materials, and incorporating plants.

The nature and design of hard surfacing should be assessed carefully for its functional and aesthetic qualities. In functional terms the surface may be used for access (for people, bikes), for children's play, for entertaining, and for sitting and sunbathing. The materials can vary widely according to function; but whatever it is used for, the best patio surface should be hard, clean, smooth, quick-drying, and weed-free. And, of course, whatever the material and the use to which it is put, it must be durable and not unreasonably expensive.

From the point of view of appearance, a potentially dull-looking hard-surfaced area can be made interesting and attractive by careful choice of colours, by breaking up the floorscape (for instance, with tubs or small beds of flowers), by changing levels, and by attention to the detailed finishing both within the surfaced area and particularly around the margins. Paving made up of small units, such as brick pavers, can both add character and create an illusion of space within a small garden. If the same type of brick is associated with materials also used in the house or its boundaries, a pleasingly co-ordinated effect may be achieved. Colours and textures are very important: bright colours that look attractive in the catalogue sometimes look garish on site, especially if they are mixed, and they tend to attract the eye away from the subtle, natural colours of your plants. Large expanses of light grey concrete are not only boring to look at but can cause glare in bright sunlight. On the other hand, lighter colours can help to reflect light into shaded areas.

The rather severe appearance of square paving can be alleviated if plantings are encouraged to overgrow the line of the edging slabs.

NATURAL STONE

York stone, limestone, granite and other kinds of natural stone have one big advantage: once laid they look instantly mellow, as if they have been in place for a long time – a good selling point if your house is an old one. But they are extremely costly, even when bought second-hand, and are not always readily available. If you are buying second-hand from a demolition yard – the cheapest source – you may find that the slabs vary greatly not only in size but in thickness too. So if you are paying a great deal for your materials it is worth shelling out still more to get a professional to lay them, rather than trying to tackle this job yourself.

PREFABRICATED SLABS

These are now the most commonly used materials for hard surfacing in the garden. Prefabricated concrete slabs are available in a vast range of colours and textures, and vary in shape from the 600 × 600mm (2 × 2ft) common grey slab to polygonal and circular forms; most of them are 50mm (2in) thick or less. More expensive types are made of reconstituted stone, and you can even find them in a texture reminiscent of

Above *Natural stone slabs, though beautifully weathered in appearance, are expensive and sometimes difficult to obtain.*

Left *Prefabricated concrete slabs are available in a variety of sizes, shapes, colours and surface textures.*

water-worn stone. It is important, however, to make sure that the surface finish is non-slip: a smooth finish encrusted with algal growth can be treacherous in wet weather. Incidentally, it is quite easy to make your own concrete paving slabs. If you construct a wooden framework from 50 × 50mm (2 × 2in) section timber with multiple 'cells' you can form several slabs at once. Prefabricated slabs come in a wide range of colours and, if you are making your own, you can colour the concrete easily with the mix-in powder. But remember not to be too heavy handed: coloured slabs when laid, and particularly when wet, tend to look brighter than they did in the builder's yard or garden centre. If you are laying a large area, it pays to use two colours, chequerboard fashion, to avoid monotony. But again, be careful in your use of combined colours. For instance, although grey and honey-beige slabs are uninteresting if used by themselves over a large area, when combined they can look very attractive.

CRAZY PAVING

Although crazy paving has often been sneered at, there is a great deal to be said for it, provided that the broken stone of which it is constructed is natural and also that it is properly laid. It is those bits of broken concrete or synthetic paving, or stretches of concrete marked out in a random pattern, or poorly fitted paving with ugly, thick mortar joints that have given crazy paving a bad name. Properly laid random paving can look perfect in a country setting, although it is inclined to seem out of place in towns or with avant-garde architecture.

Bear in mind, if you intend to use natural stone for your crazy paving, that the pieces are likely to vary considerably in thickness. This means that you must prepare the ground carefully if the paving is to present a flat, even surface.

Below *The mellow colours of old brick paving look especially good in the gardens of older properties.*

Above *Crazy paving is best made from natural stone. Although rock of a single type is safest, different colours and textures can be attractive if carefully selected.*

BRICKS

Bricks are among the most versatile of paving materials. There is an enormous range of colours and the small unit size is particularly well suited to the smaller garden. They can match the bricks used for the house and serve visually to link the house and garden and give a very pleasant appearance.

Two sorts of brick are available for garden paving. You can use standardized bricks which are frost resistant and generally, therefore, will need to be of 'special' quality. Alternatively, you can buy specially made paving bricks, which are usually thinner in section but are very hard and dense. Engineering bricks are suitable, too, but choose muted colours.

Standard bricks can be laid flat on their bedding faces or, more traditionally, you can lay them on edge (but this requires more bricks). Perforated bricks must, of course, be laid on edge. There are many bonding patterns to choose, from the simple stretcher bond to the more decorative basket weave and diagonal herringbone, but the latter pattern will entail cutting the bricks diagonally at the edges.

BLOCKS

A paving material recently introduced to this country, although it has been used for many years in continental Europe, is the concrete block, which is now available in Britain in many colours and a variety of shapes. The rectangular blocks are 200 × 100 × 65mm (8 × 4 × 2½in) in size – that is, similar in shape to, but slightly smaller than, a brick.

In the last few years too, special concrete paver blocks, in various shapes and colours, have come on the market. One of the attractions of using these is that they can be laid in a wide variety of patterns to create visual interest and sometimes also an illusion of extra space, width, or depth. They are extremely hardwearing and are usually easier for the amateur to lay than conventional bricks.

CONCRETE

Used in mass form as a garden surfacing material, concrete is hard, durable, and fairly easy to lay, and once laid it is more or less permanent. To many people, the colour of concrete is harsh, to others merely boring; certainly large, bare areas of concrete are pretty unexciting. Colouring agents can help to relieve the monotony if the concreted area is fairly small and the colours chosen with care; but a more interesting effect can be achieved by modifying the surface texture – for example, by exposing the coarse stone aggregate. Alternatively you can mark it out into mock paving squares, although, unless this is done neatly, it is likely to look worse than a plain surface. You may find that the best solution is to concentrate on stocking the surroundings with colourful plants.

A potentially gloomy conservatory can be brightened greatly by vividly coloured container-grown plants.

COBBLES

These smooth rounded stones look very attractive if you use them on a small scale, setting them around a tree for instance, or infilling an odd corner, where it might be difficult to cut larger paving materials. But they are not suitable for a large area, since they become dangerously slippery when wet, and they are totally unstable to stand garden furniture on. However, they can look very attractive when used to break up a large expanse of concrete – set in a circular swirl for instance, or ranged into a square. Granite setts, too, can be used in the same way, to provide patterns on what might otherwise be a dull expanse of paving or concrete. Bed them in carefully to achieve a flat surface.

Cube-shaped granite setts, though expensive, make a hard-wearing paved surface of distinctive colour and texture.

GRAVEL

Although it is used a great deal on the Continent, particularly in France, gravel is seldom used over here for patios, though it has many advantages. It makes a relatively inexpensive and quickly laid surfacing material. Curves are much easier to form with gravel than with paving slabs, and slight changes in level are readily accommodated. Gravel offers the advantage, too, that it can easily be taken up and later re-laid if underground piping and other services need to be installed at any time. Finally, if you become bored with it, the gravel is likely to form a good base for an alternative surface. The main disadvantage is that, unless it is carefully graded, the surface will be loose: pieces of gravel spilling on to an adjacent lawn could cause serious damage to a mower, while they are easy to bring into the house on the soles of shoes.

Gravel is available in two main forms: crushed stone from quarries, and pea gravel from gravel pits. The former is of better quality, but will be very expensive unless the stone is quarried locally. Gravel occurs in a variety of attractive natural colours, and your choice should if possible complement any stone employed in the garden for walling or rock gardens. The alternative, washed pea gravel, comes in shades from near white to almost black. Whichever type is used, ensure that the stones are neither too large (which makes walking uncomfortable), nor too small (they will stick to your shoes). For most purposes the best size is in the range 10 to 20mm ($\frac{3}{8}$ to $\frac{3}{4}$in) in diameter. Be sure that it is all of one grade; a mixture tends to settle out into layers and looks less effective.

Gravel is good at suppressing weeds. The only maintenance it should need is an occasional raking over to keep it looking trim and to remove any bumps or indentations.

DECKING

Little used in this country, but popular in the United States, decking can solve problems as an alternative to paving if you are laying a patio over several different levels or a very uneven surface. It looks particularly good in country surroundings or with modern houses and it feels pleasantly warm to walk on. But it is very expensive, and its life-span is not as great as that of concrete. You need to use hardwoods (or softwoods that have been really thoroughly treated with preservative) and the fastenings are expensive, as they must be of the very best quality. But decking is quite easy to construct yourself, unless it has to be built high off the ground, and you can get some pleasing patterns by arranging the planks in different designs. If you cannot afford to deck the entire area, see if a corner of the patio could be decked.

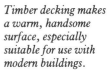
A FINAL THOUGHT ON PLANNING

You need to choose your patio surface as you would a good carpet: you are looking for something that is going to wear well, of course, but it must also be attractive to the eye and blend in with the surroundings. In other words a solid, unimaginative, grey concrete slab would detract from rather than add to the charms of a period house, whereas herringbone brick paving, or large slabs of (albeit imitation) York stone could look very attractive indeed.

If your patio is any size at all, vary the paving materials you use – don't stick to just one type. Give your patio 'professional' touches by breaking up the line of the paving, here and there, with something else – cobbles set around a newly planted tree on the patio, for instance, or small, narrow pavers outlining a large square of paving stones, or even a selection of decorative ceramic tiles (make sure they are suitable for outdoor use) forming a stone 'rug' in front of the back door. One of the easiest ways to add variety to the smaller patio is to mix small and large size slabs of the same material; most of them are made in modules that can mix so it is quite easy to do this.

If you are using slabs the easiest way to finalise your design is to buy graph paper and work it out on that. Don't feel that you have to pave the entire area; if there is space for it, why not plant a decorative tree or, at the least, a flowering bush? (But ensure that it is located where it is not going to be in the way of the main traffic runs, and where it can be seen and appreciated.) Think carefully, too, about what you are going to do with the edge of the patio, where it meets the lawn, if there is one. Avoid that 'station-platform' look at all costs by legislating for a low wall, at the very least, to finish it off.

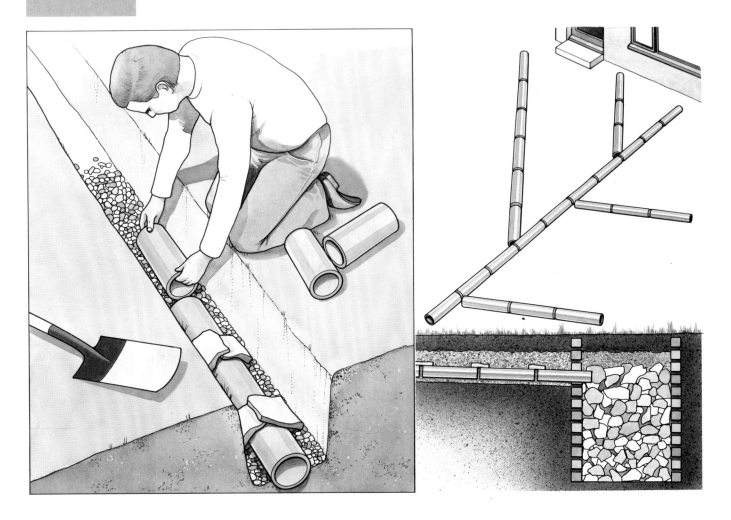

Above *Before laying paving material, make sure that the underlying surface is properly drained. The drawing at left shows installation of drainage pipes, with joints between pipe-lengths covered with slates.*

Right, above and below *A herring-bone pattern of main and tributary drainage pipes with coarse aggregate topped with finer material.*

CONSTRUCTION HINTS

Laying your own patio can be hard work. By doing so, you save a good deal of money, if not time; and for many people there is great satisfaction in doing it yourself.

Whatever form of surface you decide on, make sure that it is laid on a well-drained stable base; this will avoid problems of sinkage and water-logging. All topsoil must be removed because it contains organic matter, which will decompose and may settle. The surfacing material can sometimes be laid directly onto well-compacted subsoil, but usually a well-consolidated layer of hardcore (such as fragments of brick) is needed, covered with sand, ash, or hoggin (screened gravel).

Begin by drawing a scale plan on which are marked the lines of all the drains and the positions of manholes and water pipes. Now using manufacturer's plans and leaflets work out an appropriate layout using standard paving sizes; try to avoid having to cut slabs.

LAYING PAVING SLABS

The easiest way of laying paving slabs is to put them directly on to the soil; but this requires a light sandy soil and a comparatively level site. It is not easy to get a good level on heavy clay soils, and uneven levels can cause shifting or even cracking of the slabs. On these soils, it is best to lay the slabs on a bed of sand; this saves the effort and expense of using a mortar base.

You need a firm and level base on which to work, so first prepare the ground. Dig down deep enough to bring the finished patio to the level you want. Allow for a slight slope across the paved area to drain rainwater away from the house. If the ground is firm, you need dig out only the softer areas and replace the soil there with well-compacted hardcore. On soft clay soils, however, it's best to roll or firmly compact a 100mm (4in) thick layer of hardcore over the whole area, finishing it with a 50mm (2in) layer of sharp sand to fill in larger gaps. Mark out the edges of the patio with pegs and string to ensure that the edges of the slabs make straight lines (individual slabs vary slightly in size) and use a builder's square to make sure that your corners form right angles. Try to plan the paving in such a way that you will not have to cut any of the slabs; cutting is tricky work. Begin bedding slabs at one corner. You can lay a mortar bed under the whole of the slab; or you can lay five pads of mortar about 50mm (2in) high, one under each corner and one in the middle of the slab. Mortar used should be a 1:4 mix of cement and sand. Tap down each slab with a wooden mallet or with a hammer on a piece of softwood: treat the slabs gently to avoid breaking them. Level each slab against its neighbour and against your wooden peg reference points (which you take out progressively as work proceeds). Leave 12mm (½in) wide joints between slabs and insert wooden spacers of that width to stop the slabs closing up. Joints can be filled in various ways. You can, for instance, mix a cement/sand solution and pour it into the joints. Or you can mix the cement and sand dry (the sand needs to be very dry) and brush the dry mix into the gaps; then you sprinkle the joints with a watering can fitted with a fine rose. Generally, the easiest way is to mix up a very stiff mortar and press it firmly into the joints with the edge of a pointing trowel. Don't walk on the slabs for at least three days. If the patio is bounded by a wall at the bottom of the slope, leave a small gap between the slabs and the wall, filling the gap with pebbles to help drainage.

If your patio is going to have really heavy use, it's best to lay the slabs in a wet concrete mixture (1 part of cement to 6 of sand) at least 100mm (4in) deep. Use ready-mixed concrete to avoid hard work but make sure the site is ready when it is delivered. Guard against concrete burns by protecting your hands with gloves. The paving slabs are laid on the wet surface of the concrete after it has been tamped down and levelled.

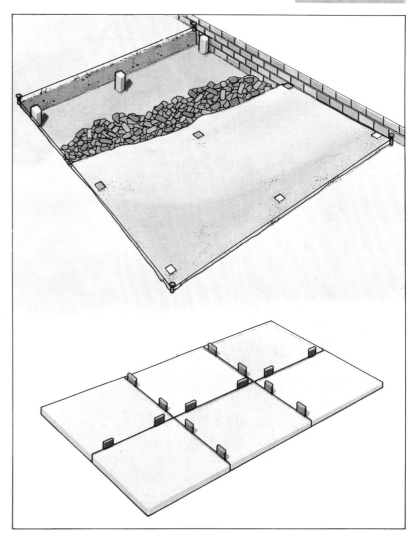

Above *Laying patio paving. In the upper picture, the site has been prepared with a sand layer over compacted hardcore; the sand surface is level with the tops of the wooden pegs, which determine the height and slope of the paving. The slabs (lower picture) are separated by spacers; the gaps are then filled with mortar.*

Left *Add interest to your hard surfacing by using more than one material.*

Solid concrete makes efficient paving – but it's a good idea to relieve its monotonous appearance with more colourful materials – and, as here, with a rich array of flowering plants.

LAYING CONCRETE

Contrary to popular belief, concrete can be laid directly on to subsoil, so long as it is firm and stable. The only preparation you need to do is to make sure the ground has the necessary slope for drainage, and then to roll it thoroughly. Any soft spots should be dug out and replaced with rammed hardcore. If the subsoil is not so suitable, prepare the ground as if you were laying paving stones, with hardcore and sand.

You will now need to set shuttering, or formwork, at the sides to keep the concrete in place when it is poured and keep it straight at the edges. Special steel shuttering and holding pins can be hired, but a cheaper alternative is to use old planks of timber, at least 25mm (1in) thick, set on their edges and held in place with pegs. Set a straight edge and spirit-level between the formwork on either side and hammer the shuttering down with a mallet until you get a level reading on the spirit level; then make fine adjustments in order to achieve a drainage slope.

Concrete is basically a mixture of cement (usually ordinary Portland cement), sharp (concreting) sand, coarse aggregate (stones), and water. For good quality concrete the proportions of these materials should be carefully measured and mixed. Always store the materials separately, and use heavy-duty plastic buckets to mea-sure the ingredients (measuring by shovelfuls is not accurate enough). Avoid laying concrete in frosty weather. The standard mixture for this type of application is 1 part of cement, 2½ parts of sharp sand, and 4 parts of 20mm (¾in) coarse aggregate.

CRAZY PAVING

Again, you need a firm base for laying, and it is generally best to lay the broken pieces of slab on to a continuous mortar bed rather than on to mortar pads; the pieces are often triangular in shape and the mortar pad method would not give enough stability for these.

The first thing to do is to sort out the larger pieces with straight edges and to lay a number of these to give you a straight line along the edges of the path or patio. Then you can infill with the smaller, irregular pieces in the middle. Howev-er, a more informal approach can also be attractive. This can be achieved by laying the paving with a deliberately ragged edge, over which trailing plants can grow. Whichever method you adopt, first lay the broken pieces loose, fitting them together in attractive com-binations of shape and colour, before you begin to fix them in their mortar bed. Try to make your paving 'jig-saw' fit as neatly as possible, so that the joints are not unattractively wide.

BRICKS

Set some sort of edging around the area – timber for instance – then lay your bricks into a 37-50mm (1½-2in) layer of mortar, leaving a 10mm (⅜in) gap between them, then grout them carefully with a dryish mix. Blocks and pavers should be set in the same way; though if arranged in interlocking patterns, they can be laid on a carefully levelled bed of sand, then bedded down with a plate vibrator.

COBBLES

These should be packed as close together as possible on a bed of mortar or concrete. Another method is to set them in a dry bed of mortar or concrete mix, then water them thoroughly with a sprinkler to set them. You can lay the cobbles at random or you can create patterns, by exploiting colour differences or by laying them in concentric circles or squares.

Far left *Brick lends itself to a huge variety of paving patterns.*

Near left *Cobbles, too, can be used to create pleasing patterns, though preferably over small areas.*

Below *Crazy paving looks best in informal settings. The site needs to be carefully prepared to ensure a level paving surface.*

Above *Formal brick
and concrete steps.*

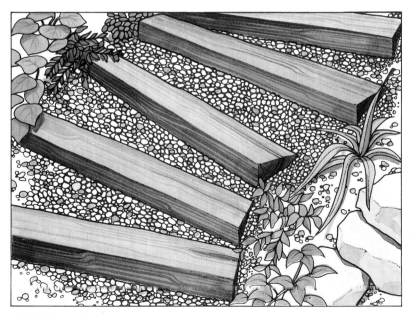

STEPS

Well-chosen, well-suited steps are more than just a necessary adjunct to a patio – they can actually enhance it if you give a little time and thought to their design. They don't have to be totally utilitarian: you could, for instance, build them with 'pockets' at either side of the treads to accommodate trailing and bedding plants, or make crevices in the risers in which you could grow alpine plants to give a waterfal of colour when viewed from below. Built-in lighting is not only a decorative trick but a safety measure, too, if you use your patio and garden at night.

The way you design your steps will depend very much on the slope that they are bridging, but there are so many attractive materials available that there is no need to make them dull. Ideally, the steps should echo or complement the material used on the patio. If the latter is paved, reserve enough additional slabs to use as the treads; the risers can be made of bricks, reproduction dry-stone walling, or any other suitable material that will blend in with a building material used elsewhere in the garden.

Discarded railway sleepers (if you can get hold of them) make interesting and unusual steps, as do rustic half-logs and old bricks; but they should not be used for a steep flight since they are all likely to become covered with algae and moss and can be slippery. If you are using paving slabs or other similar material, the flight of steps will look much more handsome if you make the treads overhang the risers by about 35mm (1½in).

Remember to keep your steps in scale with their surroundings – a grandiose sweep, complete with balustrades, would look out of place in the typical suburban garden, but there's no reason why you shouldn't have twin plinths at the top and/or bottom on which to place bowls of bedding plants.

Your first job is to work out the design of the steps on paper. Draw up cross sections from the front and from the sides to work out the number of steps that you need, for a given height of riser and a depth of tread, to fill the overall space. The area the steps cover should be twice as long as it is high. Garden steps need to be broad and shallow for safety's sake. The treads should ideally be about 375mm (15in) from front to back, and the risers 100-150mm (4-6in) high. In other words the depth of tread should be at least twice the height of the riser, and the treads should all be of equal depth, otherwise they make walking up the steps an uncomfortable business and might cause children to stumble and fall.

Left *Informal steps
made of railway
sleepers.*

CONSTRUCTING YOUR STEPS

First shape and firm the bank up which the steps are to go, cutting out the steps in the compacted soil. Then set in the first set of risers on the base. Now sit the first tread on a bed of concrete laid over a layer of hardcore. From now on each riser is set in mortar at the back of a tread, overlapping it by about 25-50mm (1-2in) to prevent the tread from tipping. Set each tread at a very slight angle, falling about 6mm (¼in) in every foot to the front or one side to allow rainwater to drain off.

Below *Garden steps, however formal, need not lack decorative qualities. These old steps down to a gloomy basement 'area' have been given colour and character merely by hanging a basket of flowers from the hand-rail.*

Above *The cut-away drawing shows a typical structure for garden steps, with brick risers and concrete-slab treads. The bottom-step risers are laid on a concrete foundation.*

PLANTING YOUR STEPS

In order to make the steps look established as soon as possible, the bank that surrounds them should be planted up quickly with basic ground cover that will give it a mature appearance. The periwinkle (*Vinca major*) grows quickly and produces pretty blue flowers in summer; or, if the area is large the bushier Rose of Sharon (*Hypericum calycinum*) gives close cover. Alternatively, ivy (*Hedera*) gives a mature look in double-quick time; and, if the steps are built alongside a retaining wall rather than a bank, ivy tumbling over the top, enlivened by ivy-leaved geraniums (*Pelargonium*) in summer, will give a very attractive display. If you do not mark your steps by pillars or some other sort of 'furniture', consider placing twin standard bay trees in tubs at the top for a formal look, or small pieces of topiary that have been grown in pots. The steps might also make a good excuse for a rose-covered arch at top or bottom; suitable arch frames which are easily assembled can be found in most garden centres.

Another idea is to make a mini-waterfall by installing parallel but narrower steps down which a greatly moving sheet of water cascades; the steps will need to be lipped at each side to avoid spillage onto either the bank or the footsteps. The water can be circulated by a pump.

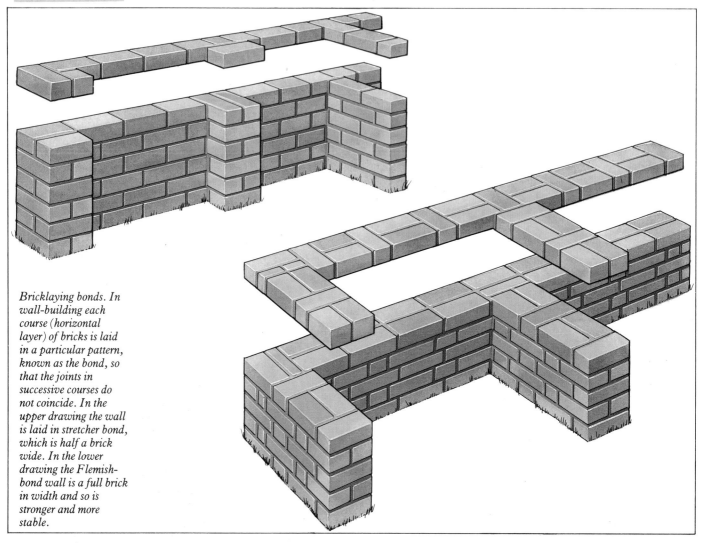

Bricklaying bonds. In wall-building each course (horizontal layer) of bricks is laid in a particular pattern, known as the bond, so that the joints in successive courses do not coincide. In the upper drawing the wall is laid in stretcher bond, which is half a brick wide. In the lower drawing the Flemish-bond wall is a full brick in width and so is stronger and more stable.

BOUNDARIES

Walls and fences do more than just act as boundaries around a patio: they give shelter against prevailing winds for both people and plants, and confer a feeling of privacy; they are also useful for screening things like dustbins and sheds. Something is often needed, too, to make a natural break between paving and grass. Although hedges can look very attractive, they take up a great deal of room, and rob the soil of nutrients for a foot or more on either side. They also need constant maintenance if they are to look trim. All things considered, a man-made barrier is usually the best solution. Solid screens made from brick or close-boarded wood are expensive but will last a long time. If you are planning a brick wall you need to dig a trench for the foundation; in the case of a fence, the posts need to be set in a concrete base.

Although a solid fence gives maximum privacy it can create considerable air turbulence on either side of it on a windy day. A more 'porous' structure may be kinder to your plants and make the patio more comfortable to sit in.

BRICK WALL

This is expensive but, once in place, will last a life-time. If you want to build your own, a low wall is certainly within the scope of the beginner. For best appearance use facing bricks, not 'commons'. Even a low wall needs a concrete foundation. As a general guide a 375mm (15in) wide strip should be excavated for a wall up to 600mm (2ft) high. Dug until firm ground is found: if stability is in doubt, lay a bed of well-compacted hardcore. Allow for a 35mm (3in) layer of concrete (1 part cement to 2½ parts sharp sand, 4 parts aggregate) with the first course of bricks to be below ground level. If the wall is to be more than 1.2m (4ft) high, lay a 100mm (4in) layer of concrete, with the first two courses of bricks below ground level. Mark out the line of the wall with two string lines pulled taut and tied to stakes. Use a mortar mix of 1 part of cement to 5 parts of builders sand. The mortar should be buttery (not too dry, nor too wet). A few drops of washing-up liquid will improve its workability, but do not mix up more mortar than you can use in an hour.

SCREEN-BLOCK WALL

This can look very attractive around a patio. It is made of precast concrete blocks, usually 300mm (1ft) square and 100mm (4in) thick. You need to provide a firm concrete foundation, using a mixture of 1 part cement to 5 parts 20mm (¾in) ballast. For the mortar use 1 part cement to 6 parts sand plus plasticizer. The foundation should be a minimum of 200mm (8in) deep, including bricks or rubble where needed. At each end of the wall, pilaster blocks are used. Loose-lay the screen blocks between the pilasters to ensure they fit, then lay the blocks as for brickwork except that you should work from both ends to the middle. Check each block for level, and again build up the corners before completing successive courses.

Drawings *Building a screen-block wall. Special pilasters (top) are built up from individual blocks. The screen blocks are laid (centre) between the pilasters, the mortar joints being strengthened by incorporating strips of expanded metal. The wall is finished (bottom) by topping off the blocks with special coping slabs and pilaster caps.*

Photographs, far left *The pierced-screen-block wall (above), though perhaps over-used in recent years, makes an efficient screen while admitting light and air. The brick wall (below) achieves a similar effect by leaving gaps between each brick in the central courses.*

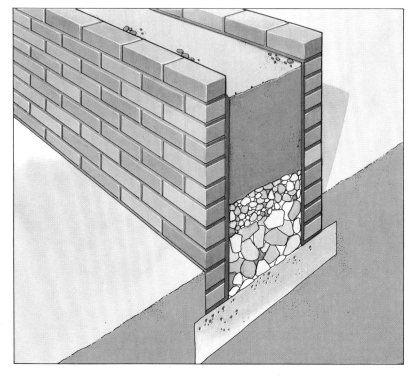

Left *A narrow raised bed, with room for colourful plantings in the cavity between the walls, makes a useful low wall to separate the patio from the rest of the garden.*

LOW WALL

If all you need is a low, decorative retaining edge to the patio, it's a good idea to build a wall made up of two parallel courses with a 150-200mm (6-8in) gap between them. You can fill the gap with soil and grow decorative plants in it. Even simpler would be a little, low wall made up of peak blocks which were interplanted with alpines and crevice plants so as to create literally a wall of flowers.

Like any other wall, it must be built on concrete foundations. Fill the bottom of the gap between the courses with rubble or hardcore.

FENCES

If you want a solid wooden fence you have a choice between closeboard or interwoven versions, both of which come as made-up panels usually 1.8m (6ft) wide and in various heights. Closeboard fencing is considerably dearer, and is often made of hard rather than soft wood. Both kinds need to be supported by posts fixed in concrete on a firm base; alternatively, you can buy special metal holders into which the posts are slotted and which spike into the ground.

RECONSTITUTED STONE

Imitation stone blocks for walling can be used to achieve the formality of a traditional dry-stone wall. The blocks should be laid on firm foundations. Use a mortar mix of 1 part of cement to 4 parts soft sand. Joints should be about 6mm (¼in) thick. If the wall is to be higher than four courses, allow a period of at least 48 hours for the mortar to harden before you begin laying the fifth and subsequent courses.

Below *This large raised bed is constructed of walling made of reconstituted-stone blocks.*

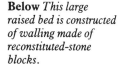

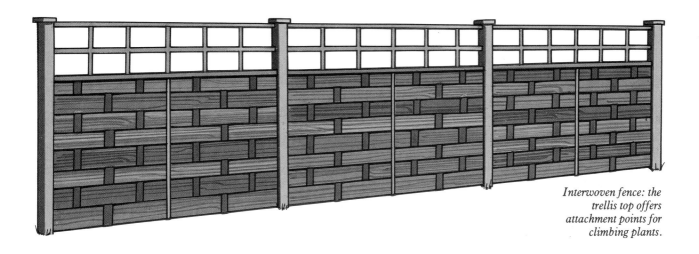

Interwoven fence: the trellis top offers attachment points for climbing plants.

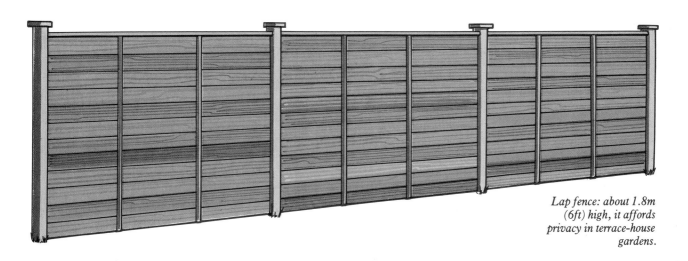

Lap fence: about 1.8m (6ft) high, it affords privacy in terrace-house gardens.

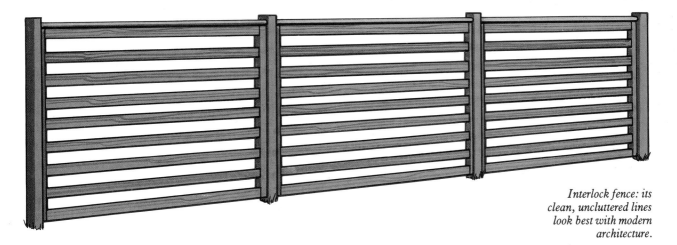

Interlock fence: its clean, uncluttered lines look best with modern architecture.

If you merely want a rudimentary screen, there is a choice of wattle fencing, trellis, or chain link, or a decorative picket fence (planks of wood spaced several inches apart fixed on rails at the top and bottom). The lighter the fencing the more important is it to make it totally secure; chain link and trellis both need some sort of frame around them if they are to stay taut. The advantage of openwork fencing is that you can decorate it quickly with climbing plants.

PATIO FEATURES

Much of the individuality of your patio will be found not so much in its basic structure as in the way you equip and furnish it for the particular uses to which it will be put. In this chapter we have a look at some of the ways to get maximum usefulness and enjoyment from your paved area.

PERGOLAS

This modern structure, combining pergola with overhead beams, represents a large open-air extension to the living room.

Add a pergola to your patio and you make it look much more like an outdoor room, for it gives an instant illusion of walls and, sometimes, a ceiling too if you include some cross-pieces overhead. It is also a useful way of showing off climbers that would otherwise be relegated to side walls.

Pergolas look impressive if built with pillars of stone or brick, but they are more usually made from timber. In that case oak or cedar are the ideal choice for uprights; but both these woods are extremely expensive, so most people use cheaper larch or pine instead. Pergolas are often available from garden centres in kit form.

MAKING YOUR OWN PERGOLA

The timber for a home-made pergola can be squared or 'rustic'. In the latter case larch poles are the best choice. Leave the bark on only if the larch has been felled during the winter; otherwise the bark will eventually fall off. It is probably better to remove it with a knife or spoke shave, and to apply varnish or a wood preservative to the underlying surface. Only butt joints are possible with rustic poles, and both joint faces must be squared before they are nailed together.

Although slim poles may look better when the pergola or arch is bare, be fairly generous with the thickness as the structure may eventually have to bear a considerable weight of foliage. Moreover, high winds, or high-spirited people swinging on the poles, can put a severe strain on the structure so err on the side of safety. Uprights should be treated like fence posts: they must be well preserved and set firmly at least 450mm (18in) in the ground. Uprights should be spaced no more than 2.4m (8ft) apart, and should not be less than 100mm (4in) in diameter or square. A variety of possibilities exists for the cross rails, but they should be a minimum of 75mm (3in) in diameter or square; a pleasing effect is produced if they extend each side of the uprights, with shaped ends. Some people who prefer a more sturdy appearance use wider but thinner cross rails, such as planking 150 × 25mm (6 × 1in). Side members should be about the same size as the cross rails, or perhaps a little smaller.

PLANTING A PERGOLA

Vines of all kinds look good when trained up a pergola; so do climbing roses, especially if they are twinned with clematis. And, if you have the space to include them, scented plants like honeysuckle (*Lonicera*) add an extra dimension of fragrance in the air when you sit out on the patio in the evening.

If the pergola forms part of an overhead structure attached to the house, it is best to train deciduous rather than evergreen climbers up it, otherwise in the winter months it may shut too much light out of the rooms nearby. Be sure to build in adequate support vine-eyes and wires before you plant your climbers: it is much easier to do it at that stage than when you have to struggle with fully grown plants. If, for some reason, you cannot have ordinary beds around the base of the pergola – for instance, the support poles may be built into the patio itself – then a series of rectangular troughs could be fitted around the base of the supports instead and planted with shallow-rooting climbers. For a permanent planting, wisteria looks very attractive, while if you need quick cover you can't beat the Russian vine or mile-a-minute (*Polygonum baldschuanicum*), though it will need frequent and fairly ruthless cutting back once established if it is not to take over.

This simple lean-to pergola offers ample support even for a large, mature climber.

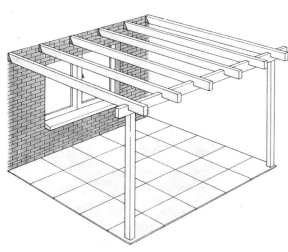

Basic design for a pergola and overhead beams. The vertical posts must be sunk at least 900mm (3ft) into concrete foundations beneath the paving. The overhead beams shown here are made from 150×50mm (6×2in) floor joists; at the house end they slot into joist hangers set into the wall.

BARBECUE DESIGNS & SITES

If you are constructing a patio, why not build in a barbecue at the same time? It will cost very little – you probably have the materials to hand – and, apart from being something of a status symbol, it's great fun to use when the weather is kind.

Choose a sheltered spot on which to site it – you don't want a howling wind fanning the flames, and make sure that it is away from precious shrubs or climbers; evergreens, on the whole, stand up better than deciduous shrubs to being scorched occasionally. The ideal site is against a brick or concrete wall, where it can do little or no harm. If this is not possible (the walls of the house are not suitable because of smoke drifting indoors), then consider making an island site for it on the patio, if there is space; then everyone can gather round and help (or hinder) the cook. Keep it reasonably near the kitchen so that dishes and foodstuffs can be shuttled back and forth without too long a walk.

You can now buy barbecue kits which can be built in as a permanent fixture. They consist of a grid and tray to take the charcoal and a grill on which to put the food. An attractive extra is a battery-operated rotisserie which fits over the top. This equipment is incorporated into a simple three-sided brick wall which anyone can make and which requires only a little over 100 bricks. Alternatively, you can buy an attractive small triangular barbecue kit that will go into an odd corner and occupy little usable space.

If you have the space, it pays to build two more brick piers at either side of your barbecue and continue the bricks at the back, then to fix ceramic tiles on a wooden base on top. You then have an area on either side on which to prepare and serve food. Cupboards can be built underneath, not only to house charcoal and other cooking items, but the odd flower pot or two as well.

Make the most of your barbecue. Plant essential herbs around it so that guests can help themselves to flavourings – mint, tarragon, and especially chives can then be snipped over salads, while fennel goes well with fish, and lamb is particularly good when cooked over rosemary. The herbs can be grown in tubs as part of the decoration of the patio, or in a specially raised bed nearby.

Remember that you will need some good lighting so that the cook can see what he or she is doing. A discreet spotlight set high will do the trick or you could floodlight the whole area.

CONSTRUCTING A BASIC BARBECUE

Set the bricks out, dry, on the patio where the barbecue is to be, making two courses. Then, using the barbecue grill as a guide, check that the dimensions are correct and square, and draw a line around the inside of them as your guide.

Then mix up your mortar so that it is workable and not runny, adding a spot of

A built-in barbecue with storage cupboard. The barbecue grill can be adjusted for height. The cupboard has quarry tiles on top to provide a durable working surface.

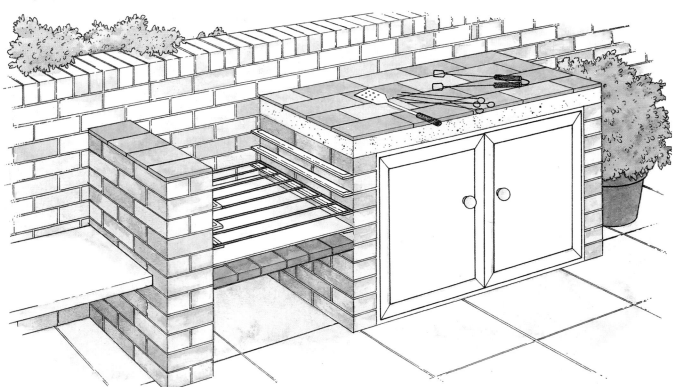

A barbecue/storage cupboard design basically similar to that on the opposite page. For alfresco meals a table can be used with the L-shaped seating built into the brick structure.

washing-up liquid to it, to make it easier to work. Lay the bricks along the back wall first, then add the side wall bricks, checking all the time against your pencil guide, making sure they are square and level. Then start the second course – the corner bricks will have to be placed to make a half bond – and continue round, ending with two half bricks to finish off the front at either side. When you get to the height where the charcoal tray is to go, put three bricks sideways on so that they project as half-bricks from the centre of each side wall, to form a ledge on which the tray can sit. An average barbecue is 11 courses high, but you can vary it to suit yourself.

A more elaborate barbecue could be constructed, Spanish style, with a brick arch overhead, culminating in a chimney. This sort of thing would become a focal point of the patio and should be treated accordingly; the wall at the back could be covered in decorative tiles, and lighting could play its part in adding drama to the setting (wrought-iron outdoor lamps can be found that would go very well in this scheme).

To extend the usefulness of a barbecue beyond the summer season, consider the possibility of building some sort of overhead protection against the weather. A pergola could be extended and roofed in, for instance; and provided the barbecue itself had an arch and chimney over it, or some other method of avoiding a fire hazard, you could eat alfresco for many more evenings of the year.

A simple mini-pool designed to have an informal, pond-like appearance.

MINI POOLS

Water brings instant magic to a patio. It's infinitely soothing to jaded nerves to sit beside a small pool on a hot summer's day, with nothing more strenuous to do than watch the fish, or listen to the trickle of a bubbling fountain. A pool is like a mirror, too, reflecting the sky, and making the patio seem larger than it really is.

Most patio pools, nowadays are home-made with the help of butyl rubber liners or bought in pre-formed shapes made from fibreglass. Choose a pool size and shape to suit your particular setting. Generally, straight lines in a patio dictate a square or rectangular pond. It is a good idea to incorporate a pond into the patio design at construction stage, leaving out a square or two of paving, perhaps, or building a brick container to hold it above ground level; 450-650mm (18-30in) is the usual height. The irregular outlines of the free-form fibreglass pools that can be bought readymade are usually better used in a rockery setting or cut into a lawn; but almost anything water-tight can make a pond – even a discarded bath, so long as you hide its all too obvious edges. Bowls, sinks, urns or tubs, even if they are cracked and leaky, make a good basis for a pool, since they can be lined with butyl (obtainable from garden centres).

Be careful where you site your pool. It's best kept away from trees, especially deciduous ones, because rotting leaves in the autumn can cause pollution of the water. And your pool should receive direct sunlight for at least half the day.

MAKING A POND

If you decide to dig your own pond, mark it out first with string and pegs. When you shape the sides, cut them in one or more steps with sloping sides rather than as a single vertical drop; then you can use extra marginal plants, and the walls are less likely to fall in. To calculate the amount of pond liner needed, measure the length and width of the pond and add twice the depth to each measurement. For example, if your pool is 600 × 900mm (2 × 3ft) and 300mm (1ft) deep, you will need a sheet of butyl 1.2 × 1.5m (4 × 5ft) in size. Line the hole first, to avoid puncturing the butyl. An old piece of carpet or carpet underlay will do, or pieces of turf. Put the butyl in place in warm weather, when it will be more pliable and will cling to the curves of the hole you have excavated.

Begin filling the pool slowly with a hose. The liner will gradually sink. Ease it down until it fits snugly. Try to smooth out wrinkles as they occur, although most should have disappeared by the time the pool is full of water. When the pool is full, trim off the waste liner material, leaving about 200mm (8in) around the edge at the top for fixing down. In corners and tight bends make sure the sheeting does not get bunched – it must be folded over neatly to hide the surplus; never cut out segments of spare material, as this will almost certainly cause the liner to tear later on.

The edge of the butyl liner is best hidden under paving stones – an easy job if you are incorporating it into the patio. You can leave little pockets of soil around the edges and plant pond-site trailing plants. Make sure that your paving laps over the edge of the pool, to hide the liner exposed above the waterline.

It is important to keep your pool as clean as you possibly can. The best way to do this is to instal oxygenating plants, such as water moss (*Fontinalis antipyretica*), spiked water milfoil (*Myriophyllum spicatum*), which has delicate fine-toothed leaves, and Canadian pond-weed (*Elodea canadensis*). Water lilies (*Nymphaea*) look exotic but they are surprisingly easy to grow. Once they are anchored in place they need little or no attention. A number of lilies will grow very happily in tub pools; for example, *N. nitida*, which has cup-shaped flowers which appear in early summer. If you are planning a really small pond there are small water lilies that you can use; look for the name *N. pygmaea*. Pigmy lilies in shallow water need bringing indoors in the winter if there is a sharp frosty spell. If the plants cannot be moved, cover the pool with a wooden board in cold weather. Water lilies should be planted in May or June.

FOUNTAINS

A fountain not only gives a vertical dimension to a pool but focuses interest, and creates a feeling of coolness on a hot day. It also helps to oxygenate the water – important if you have fish. Be careful to buy a pump of the right size. One that is too powerful will send the spray shooting all over the patio. Even when the nozzle is turned right down; it will also disturb water-lilies and may affect their growth.

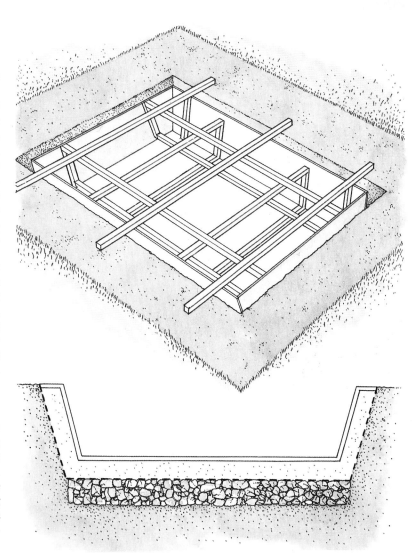

Above *Constructing a concrete pool. After the pool floor has been laid, this framework enables the side walls to be formed; the concrete is poured into the space between the wooden shuttering and the surrounding earth.*

Left *A fountain can be operated by a simple pump recirculating the pool water.*

Right *On a small patio, built-in benching is a space-saving alternative to chairs and loungers.*

Opposite page *These simple slatted chairs can be folded for compact storage.*

Below *One of Marks and Spencer's ranges of patio furniture. The sunshade can be tilted and adjusted for height.*

PATIO FURNITURE

The first thing you have to decide, when choosing furniture for your patio, is whether it is to stay out all year round or be stored away in winter. Furniture that can be left out of doors is made from wood – usually hardwood – plastic or metal. Furniture that must be taken indoors is made from cane or bamboo, unpainted and untreated softwood and, of course, anything that is upholstered. Storing garden furniture indoors or in a garage can sometimes present problems, unless you buy something that can actually be used as indoor furniture too. But there is a third category – items like loungers, chairs and tables that are collapsible or can be easily dismantled, and take up very little space when stored.

Choose your furniture to go with the style of your house and patio. Rustic, rough-hewn benches and tables usually look out of place in a town setting, unless you have deliberately created a country garden look to go with them. Bamboo and cane look good with 'tropical' plants like the yucca, but they are less happy in stark modern surroundings. Wooden furniture should be strongly made, especially if it is to stay outside all year round. Check that any metal screws, hinges or fittings on them are made from stainless steel or brass rather than steel, which will rust. Plastic furniture, including that made

from glass-fibre, is usually trouble free, but it should be heavy enough to be stable so that it will not topple over easily.

Metal furniture ranges from antique reproductions in cast aluminium to stackable folding chairs in bright colours and modern designs. Cast aluminium chairs and tables are expensive to buy but last indefinitely and will not rust. Most other metals need to be painted regularly unless they have been enamelled or coated with plastic. Most of the better-quality metal furniture has the disadvantage of being heavy to move around, so it is better chosen for a large patio, where it can stay permanently in place.

Upholstered chairs and loungers – and there are some very sumptuous ones around – and swing seats should all have detachable cushions. Even so, it's a good idea to have a rainproof cover of some sort for the larger items so that, should there be a sudden shower, you can quickly shield them from it, rather than have to pull off canopies and cushions and bring them inside.

If you have the space for it, it's a good idea to build in some of your patio furniture. A very attractive bench-seat can be constructed, for instance, around a large tree, or an arbour with a seat built into it can be established in a corner of the patio. But it is for dining that built-in furniture really comes into its own. A brick-built bench seat along one wall, and possibly going round a corner too, takes up far less space than a set of chairs. It can be made in several different ways: it could have a hinged wooden seat, for instance, which lifts up to reveal storage space for garden tools; or it could have a tiled top with cupboards underneath. A brick-built bench of this kind could have two deep troughs built into it at each end in which you could plant flowers.

A built-in table can be made quite simply if you can get hold of a very large piece of slate or marble that would make a top; these can sometimes be picked up in junk shops. Two simple brick piers usually suffice to take the place of legs, or, if the table top is very small, you might be able to get away with just one acting as a central plinth.

Junk shops are also a source of temporary patio furniture – things like old kitchen chairs and tables – which you can get for a very low price. Unified by a coat of bright paint – bright blue, green, or scarlet, for instance – several odd chairs will go together perfectly happily, an old table, perhaps with a laminated plastic top, can be painted to match; then cover the painted top with a heavy sheet of glass to keep it good-looking. Indoor furniture that has been thoroughly painted should last outdoors for a year or so; though if the joints are glued they may need re-doing after a time.

DESIGNING FOR CHILDREN

A patio that is going to be used by children needs careful thought, at the planning stage, so that it can lead a useful life throughout the day and, eventually, revert to being purely ornamental as the family grows up. With play in mind, the basic structure of the patio should offer as few hazards as possible. It might be better, for instance, to provide access by a ramp instead of shallow steps to the garden to facilitate use of tricycles and other wheeled toys.

If the patio is large enough to take it, it would be a good idea to provide one corner especially for the children. If enough play space and attractions are concentrated in this area, it may reduce the temptation to run wild in the more precious ornamental areas. Storage could also be built along one wall to park toys that could be kept permanently out of doors, to avoid having to trundle them into the house.

When you are providing facilities for the children, use a little cunning and site them so that they can be adapted, later on, for other uses. A sand-pit could be built into the patio itself by leaving out some of the paving in a square, rectangular, or even free-form shape. (If you do this, line the bottom of the pit with un-mortared bricks to allow drainage.) Then, when the family have grown up it can be turned into an attractive ornamental pond, or a bed for flowers or herbs. If the sand-pit is of a regular shape and not too large, you could build a simple box-like structure to go on top of it when not in use. This would not only keep the rain and family pets out, but would act as a simple seat, made more attractive by addition of brightly coloured cushions. A sand-pit can also make a convenient spot to site the holder for a whirlygig washing line, so that its pole can be slotted in and out when needed.

If the children have their own corner, it's a good idea to encourage their interest in plants at an early stage by giving them some growing space of their own. Packets of annual flowers, generously sprinkled on the soil, covered and watered, usually oblige, but children also enjoy growing novelty things. The sensitive plant (*Mimosa pudica*) can be grown as an annual (it won't survive a winter out of doors) and its leaves fold up, instantly, if you touch them. The squirting cucumber (*Ecballium elaterium*) literally fires its seeds at you as if from a gun. And gourds, decorative squashes and the loofah plant are all interesting curiosities for children to grow. On the edible front, radishes grow with amazing speed, provided they are well watered, and vegetable spaghetti (a marrow with flesh that looks just like spaghetti when you cook it) is well worth trying. Tiny tomatoes like 'Gardener's Delight' are also fun for children, as are alpine strawberries, used for ground cover.

For the rest of the patio, it's best to plant a framework of trees and shrubs on and around it that are relatively child-proof. But this doesn't mean that you have to give up flowers: viburnums, olearias, philadephus, and shrub roses will give you an attractive range of flowers and foliage, while shrubs with coloured foliage such as the purple-leaved hazel (*Corylus maxima* 'Purpurea'), the golden elder (*Sambucus nigra* 'Aurea'), or the smoke tree (*Cotinus coggygria*) will provide colourful focal points all through the summer. With a boisterous family it is better to legislate for some degree of accidental damage and plant multi-stemmed trees such as birch (*Betulus*), alder (*Alnus*), or hornbeam (*Carpinus betulus*) so that even if part of the tree is injured, the rest will survive to form an attractive clump.

A children's sand-pit made from railway sleepers. Secured by a vertical bolt at each corner, the timber walls are less painful to young shins and knees than brick or concrete.

PLANTS POISONOUS TO CHILDREN
Aconite, aquilegia, box (*Buxus*), cotoneaster, daphne, beech (*Fagus sylvatica*), hellebore, iris, ivy (*Hedera*), juniper (*Juniperus*), laburnum, oleander, and pulsatilla are a few among many.

PATIO LIGHTING

Lighting, if it is properly used, can completely change the look and atmosphere of your patio at night. At the touch of a switch the whole scene is illuminated, and you are in control. You can draw attention to the things that you want people to see, such as flowering plants, an attractively shaped specimen tree, a climber in bloom, and leave items such as dustbins or an untidy bed in darkness.

There are several different types of lights to choose from, depending on the effect that you want to make. Floodlights can be fixed to light up the entire patio area or to illuminate one end wall. They are usually fixed high up on the house itself and angled. Spotlights give a far more intimate effect and are usually fixed on brackets on a wall or on spikes that you can

insert into a flower bed. They are very effective for drawing attention to one particular item – a statue, for instance, or a tree or plant with striking foliage. They can also be used as down-lighting over a barbecue so that the cook can work more easily.

LIGHTING PONDS
Moving water is the most spectacularly rewarding of all patio features when lit up after dark. By far the best effects come from submerged lamps – which must, of course, be a type made specifically for that purpose. Water looks at its best lit from below and behind. A lamp shining up behind a fountain, for instance, turns it into a rippling sheet of molten coloured glass.

TEMPORARY LIGHTS
Candles in barbecue lanterns or jamjars can make attractive occasional or temporary lighting if you are eating outdoors. Giant church candles are also excellent and they are stable enough to be stood on their own on the patio floor. Coloured flares and nightlights, which are now obtainable almost everywhere, give the patio a gala look and are particularly good for parties. They are generally available on thin canes.

Far left *Examples of exterior lighting. Halogen bulbs have allowed the introduction of more powerful lamps for garden use.*

Near left *Imaginatively sited, patio lights can achieve delightful effects.*

PLANTS FOR THE PATIO

The fact that patios are essentially hard-paved areas need place few restrictions on the range of plants you wish to choose to decorate the area. Large shrubs and even trees will grow happily in containers, and climbers can be trained up walls or pergolas and along overhead beams. In this chapter we look at some of the best plants for different sites on the patio.

Far right *A massive wine jar plays host to* Clematis macropetala *'Maidwell Hall'.*

CONTAINERS

Containers of all kinds – pots, tubs, troughs and home-built raised beds – are the basic furnishings of the patio, your outdoor room. With their help you are able to have colour all year round, arranging it in different ways according to your whim. There is no heavy digging to do; you will not even have to bend down if your containers are sited high enough; there is little or no weeding to worry about; and you are less troubled by weather conditions than in a conventional plot. You can suit yourself as far as soil is concerned, filling some containers with the acid kind for lime-hating plants such as rhododendrons and azaleas, and others with chalky soil, which such favourites as aster, clematis and lilac love. In short, you have the best of all gardening worlds.

You can also shift your garden around in any way you want, provided that you have made sure that your containers are movable. You can give them each a turn to have their fair share of the sun. You can tuck ones that have finished flowering behind the others, or use planted containers to hide an attractive feature. Plan your containers for bold massed effect. It is more labour-saving to put several plants into one large container rather than have the same number singly in an array of pots. They grow better together, they need watering less frequently, and they make a greater visual impact: one large tub looks more impressive and takes up less space than half a dozen flower pots huddled together.

Right *A tub crammed with a fine display of the 'Resisto Rose' variety of petunia.*

TUBS, POTS AND TROUGHS

These are made in several different kinds of material and it is important to choose the material that suits both you and your garden. Plastic saves the most labour and it is usually cheapest, too. It is lightweight, colour-fast, and, unless it gets cracked or torn, will last for a long time, although it tends to get brittle after several years in the sunlight. Plants in such containers need watering less often than those in conventional clay pots, from which moisture evaporates through the walls. Plastic containers are now made in some attractive classic shapes; they range in appearance from imitation wood to plain white and some good colours, too. If you do not like the colours, it is easy to repaint plastic pots using acrylic-based paints. Glass-fibre containers are expensive, but should, if handled properly, last for a life-time. If you want a 'period' look for your pots, this is your best choice, as glass-fibre can be used to simulate any container material, from wood to lead.

Stone, artificial stone, and concrete containers look very attractive, but they are very heavy, so you should be sure where you want to site them before you plant them up. They are expensive, too, and tend to be fragile: they may crack in a heavy frost or crumble with age, so they should never be moved unless it is absolutely necessary to do so.

Terracotta pots, including the traditional flower pot, look and feel good, but they too are expensive and tend to break easily, and their plants need watering frequently. Plants grown in such containers are also more likely to have their roots affected by frost, so they need more attention, and it is a good idea to protect them in really cold weather. With all these drawbacks, however, terracotta pots are most people's favourite containers: plants somehow look *right* in them. Wooden containers are also very attractive, but they will deteriorate over a period of time, however thoroughly you paint them or treat them with preservative. Wood is invaluable for purpose-built-containers – a specially made box to fit an awkwardly shaped window-sill, for instance, or a wooden tub to fit over a manhole cover. Wooden tubs or half barrels are fairly heavy; they also lose water easily – in summer a tub on a hot patio may need watering two or even three times a day.

Below *A half-barrel with calceolaria (yellow), heliotropium (purple) and zonal pelargonium (red) – a delightful mixture of flower and foliage colours completed by the splash of campanula (lilac) growing on the ground besides the container.*

Above *A trough made of natural stone makes a fine container in formal gardens of older houses.*

HANGING BASKETS

The containers mentioned so far are placed on the patio floor. Hanging baskets are particularly useful because they create centres of interest at or above eye level. Half baskets can be hung on walls; full baskets can be suspended from wall brackets or from beams. But remember that when large baskets are filled they are heavy, so wall or beam fixings must be suitably strong.

Baskets should be lined with tightly-packed sphagnum moss, a cellulose liner or black polythene. If moss is used, a saucer should be placed on the layer of moss at the bottom to provide a reservoir of water – life-saving in hot weather. Watering can be a problem. Baskets dry out quickly when exposed to sun and wind, and need to be watered daily during the summer. It may be necessary to take the basket down once a week for a good soak; and a syringe with water each evening in hot weather will be appreciated.

Far right, above
Hanging baskets are useful and decorative spacesavers on a small patio. This one sports nasturtiums (orange), pelargoniums (red and white), and lobelias (pink).

Above *The window box at right (crowded with pelargoniums and lobelias) is fine for sash-windows sills. For outward-opening casement windows, however, something else is needed. One answer is a row of easily movable pots, as in the picture at left.*

CONVERSIONS AND HOME-MADES

If you want to get away from purpose-built containers and look for something interestingly unconventional in which to house your plants, the range is enormous. Anything from a cocoa tin to an old domestic cold-water tank can be used to hold plants. Surprisingly large trees can be grown on the patio in containers too – you could even have a mini-orchard provided you fed the fruit trees well.

There's no end to the items you can press into service: old kitchen coppers make very attractive plant containers, as do cisterns which can often be found abandoned on skips. Pots and pans that have outlived their usefulness make good portable containers and you can paint them in vivid colours or decorate them, narrow-boat style, in bright patterns. Canteen-size kettles make good plant holders, and so do outsize teapots. It pays to look around second-hand shops for items that are chipped or cracked and knocked down for a few pence which might make attractive plant holders.

Chimney pots are so well known now in their new guise as plant containers that you may have to pay over the odds for them. But if you are lucky enough to secure one, it is more sensible to sit a large flower-pot in the top of it, rather than fill the entire chimney pot with soil. If you want to mass a number of plants together, a small wooden wheelbarrow makes a good display piece, or an old tin hip bath. Even a dolls' pram can be used as a plant holder: give it a good coat of paint first and it should last several seasons. On the fun front, discarded wellies or climbing boots make amusing temporary homes for plants, such as spring bulbs, that are to sit on a window sill.

Old kitchen sinks make good troughs for small plants such as alpines. Stone sinks can be left as they are, but china ones look better if you give them a rough-cast treatment. Spread them first with an impact-bonding PVA glue (you will need rubber gloves for this job), then pat on a mixture of Portland cement, sand and peat, in proportions of 1:2½:1½, over the sides and leave it to dry. Do not try to put on too much rough cast at a time. The best way is to build up the thickness of the coating by making several applications, allowing the rough cast to dry between each thickness. The same technique could be used for any ceramic object; an old, large mixing bowl, for instance, could very easily be turned into a rough-cast plant pot.

If cash is limited, you can save your money for the plants, rather than spend it on containers, by copying the French and Italians. Collect together the largest paint cans you can find and spray or paint them all the same colour with lacquer (dazzling turquoise blue looks particularly effective). Before you plant them up, make drainage holes in the bottom.

You may be lucky enough to lay your hands

A section of a dead tree trunk makes a pleasantly informal plant container.

on a cheap, large tub or a half-barrel to grow plants in. Strawberry barrels are well known, but there is no reason why you should not plant them up with flowers instead; they look particularly good if you mix bedding plants with trailers like sweet peas (*Lathyrus odoratus*) or nasturtiums (*Tropaeolum*). To plant up a barrel effectively, place a piece of drainpipe down over the centre as you fill it, and fill the pipe with gravel or small stones, pulling it up as you go. This gives the barrel a central draining system.

One of the best ways of getting the kind of container you want is to build a raised bed for your plants. You can then have exactly the right dimensions and, provided the soil is topped up from time to time with fertiliser, it is a permanent fixture. Small plants like alpines can be viewed more easily when raised above ground level. You can use a number of materials other than brick – stone, baulks of timber, or peat blocks. But if you use wood, it must first be treated with a non-toxic preservative.

The larger and higher the bed, the more secure the foundations will have to be. A low bed can just be constructed on the patio floor. The front wall should have a slight backward slope, to help to contain the earth inside. It must have drainage holes in it; insert pieces of tubing between courses of brick, stone, or timber near the bottom of the bed so that excess water can drip out.

The austere lines of Versailles tubs (here with petunias and lobelias) lend themselves to formal settings.

SMALL-SPACE EVERGREEN SHRUBS AND PERENNIALS

Acaena	Escallonia	Osmanthus
Arbutus	Eucalyptus	Pachysandra
Arundinaria	Eucryphia (some)	Pernettya
Aucuba	Euonymus (some)	Phlomis
Berberis (some)	Euphorbia (some)	Phormium
Bergenia (most)	× Fatshedera	Photinia
Buxus	Fatsia	Picea
Calluna	Festuca	Pieris
Camellia	Fremontodendron	Pyracantha
Ceanothus (some)	Garrya	Rhododendron
Chamaecyparis	Gaultheria	(many)
lawsoniana	Hebe	Rosmarinus
dwarf forms	Hedera	Ruscus
Choisya	Hypericum (some)	Ruta
Cistus	Iberis	Santolina
Convolvulus cneorum	Ilex	Sarcococca
Cotoneaster (some)	Juniperus	Senecio (most)
Cryptomeria	Kalmia (some)	Skimmia
× *Cupressocyparis*	Laurus	Taxus
leylandii	Leptospermum	Teucrium
'Castlewellan'	Ligustrum (some)	Thuja
Daboecia	Lonicera (some)	Thymus
Daphne (some)	*Magnolia grandiflora*	Trachycarpus
Elaeagnus	Mahonia	Viburnum (some)
Embothrium	Myrtus	Vinca
Erica	Olearia	Yucca

Above, right
Evergreen Fatsia japonica, *with its white October flowers, makes a good permanent resident in sun or shade.*

Right *Make a virtue of necessity by building a patio around an awkwardly sited tree. The speckled shade cast by its foliage will be a boon on hot summer days.*

DECORATIVE PLANTS

PERMANENT RESIDENTS

The long-term inhabitants of the patio need to be chosen with care, as they are to be planted in a small space – but that does not mean that they need to be dull. Evergreen, for instance, does not necessarily have to be green: there are many attractive shrubs and small trees whose foliage comes in golden or variegated versions; holly (*Ilex*) and box (*Buxus*) provide several examples. Some of the *Chamaecyparis* species (including the familiar Lawson's cypress) have dwarf varieties bearing gold, silvery blue, or purplish foliage; while some heathers (*Calluna*) are yellow all year round. Many of the hebes have leaves with white or cream edges, as does the variegated form of Japanese spurge (*Pachysandra terminalis*).

When you are looking through catalogues of shrubs and perennials, make a point of checking to see if there are variegated as well as plain versions of the plants you are interested in. Variegated or golden foliage looks particularly good if the patio is dark and shady, as it will tend to light it up. A good evergreen for shade, incidentally is the false castor-oil plant (*Fatsia japonica* 'Variegata') whose huge, glossy green leaves with white tips look very exotic. Resembling an indoor rather than an outdoor plant, it goes well with plants like the yucca if you are giving your patio a tropical look.

Rhododendrons and camellias, with their

elegant dark green leaves, are useful additions to the patio because of the shapely, vividly coloured flowers that they also bring. Rhododendrons, especially the smaller azalea forms, are a good choice because they are shallow rooting and therefore suitable for raised beds and tubs; but remember that rhododendrons must be planted in acid soil – they are lime-haters.

Having got your backdrop installed, there are a number of attractive perennials that can be put in place as further furnishings to add interest all year round. Rosemary and lavender will add fragrance, and, like sage (*Salvia*) and thyme, are useful herbs to have around. Go for variety in colour and shape with your perennial plants – contrasting, for instance, the deep-cut silvery leaves of wormwood (*Artemisia absinthium*) with the round, golden-green leaves of lady's mantle (*Alchemilla mollis*) together with the sword-like spikes of New Zealand flax (*Phormium tenax*). You should aim at a mix of tall spiky and round hummocky plants, and a range of foliage colours from near golden yellow to the silver shades and blue-greens.

Make bulbs part of your overall scheme, for in a small space nothing gives better value for money year after year. Plant daffodils (*Narcissus*) tulips, and crocuses in clumps rather than strung out in rows: they look much more effective when massed together. And have at least one tub crammed with colour in this way in spring. If you have a raised bed or two, then consider growing the tiny species bulbs as well, they look wonderful mixed with alpines. Remember that you can have bulbs in flower in the autumn too, if you plant in early summer. The autumn crocus (*Colchicum*) has crocus-like flowers almost as big as those of tulips; they come up on bare stalks, however, so they need to be mixed in with something else – the silvery sea ragwort (*Senecio cineraria*) makes a particularly good foil for them (it is, however, not fully hardy and is usually treated as an annual). Later on the nerines, those beautiful pink 'lilies' from South Africa, will reward you with their delicate colour from early autumn almost up to Christmas.

Plants for shade

Acanthus
Aconitum
Anemone
Aquilegia
Astrantia
Aucuba
Begonia
Bergenia
Berberis
Camellia
Convallaria
Cotoneaster simonsii
Digitalis
Euonymus radicans
Forsythia
Galanthus
Helleborus
Hosta
Hydrangea
Hypericum
Impatiens
Kerria japonica
 'Pleniflora'
Lilium
Lysimachia
Phlox
Primula
Pyracantha
Rhododendron (Azalea)
Ribes sanguineum
Saxifraga umbrosa
Skimmia japonica
Vinca
Viola

Above, left *The vibrant colours of many azaleas deserve a special position on the patio.*

Plant	Planting time	Depth	Flowering time	Height
Acidanthera	May	75mm (3in)	July-Oct	450-600mm (18-24in)
Anemone ('De Caen' ànd 'St Brigid' strains)	Spring	50mm (2in)	June-Sept	200-300mm (8-12in)
Begonia	May	50mm (2in)	July-Oct	200-250mm (8-10in)
Brodiaea	March-April	75-100mm (3-4in)	June-July	400-500mm (16-20in)
Dahlia	After last frost	75-100mm (3-4in)	Aug-Oct	300-1500mm (1-5ft)
Freesia	From mid-Apr	50mm (2in)	July-Sept	200-250mm (8-10in)
Galtonia	Apr	100mm (4in)	July-Aug	900-1200mm (3-4ft)
Gladiolus:				
small-flowered	Apr-June	75mm (3in)	June-July	450mm (18in)
large-flowered	Apr-June	75mm (3in)	July-Sept	1.5m (5ft)
Hymenocallis	May-June	125-150mm (5-6in)	July-Aug	450mm (18in)
Lilium	Feb-Apr	100-125mm (4-5in)	June-Sept	600-1500mm (2-5ft)
Montbretia (syn. Crocosmia)	Apr-May	50mm (2in)	July-Sept	400mm (16in)
Ornithogalum	Mar-Apr	50mm (2in)	Aug-Oct	300-350mm (12-14in)
Oxalis	Apr-May	50mm (2in)	July-Sept	100-150mm (4-6in)
Ranunculus	Mar-May	50mm (2in)	June-Aug	250mm (10in)
Sparaxis	Apr	50mm (2in)	June-July	200mm (8in)
Sprekelia	Apr	100mm (4in)	June	450-600mm (18-24in)
Tigridia	Mar-Apr	75mm (3in)	July-Aug	400mm (16in)

Left *A selection of summer-flowering bulbs. Use them with larger permanent residents to provide additional colour in tubs and troughs.*

proposition for, say, a pergola where you want overhead leaves, and its long delicate racemes of white flowers hang down in an attractive way. It is a good idea to team it with a slower-growing, more attractive climber, such as a grape-vine or wisteria, provided you keep it under control. Two other rapid climbers to look for are varieties of *Clematis montana* and *Rosa filipes* 'Kiftsgate', a very vigorous rambler with huge trusses of white flowers that will eventually need checking.

Some climbers are self-supporting and do not need help in the form of netting or wires. Those valued mainly for foliage include common ivy, Boston ivy (*Parthenocissus tricuspidata* 'Veitchii') and Virginia creeper (*P. quinquefolia*). Climbing roses, on the whole, can look after themselves and just need fastening here and there against the wall. They make a marvellous show, but they should be sited with care in a very small space, as their thorns may become a nuisance.

Clematis and other 'softer' climbers, such as winter jasmine (*Jasminum nudiflorum*) and honeysuckle (*Lonicera*), need plenty of wire, netting or trellis to cling to and climb over and to protect them from strong winds. But they do tend to make fast growth and flower quickly and they do not need tying in. They can also be grown easily in pots, as can passion flower (*Passiflora caerulea*), which actually flowers better if it has some root restriction. If you are planning on climbers for pergolas and posts

The slower-growing climber wisteria (above) contrasts with aptly named mile-a-minute or Russian vine (right).

Climbers for the patio

Akebia
Campsis
Celastrus
Clematis
Cobaea
Eccremocarpus
Hedera
Hydrangea petiolaris
Ipomoea
Jasminum
Lathyrus
Lonicera
Parthenocissus
Passiflora
Polygonum
Rosa
Solanum
Tropaeolum
Wisteria

CLIMBERS

You can almost double the potential growing space of your patio if you use the boundary walls in an imaginative way by planting them with climbers. Moreover, it's a good way to 'tie in' the walls of the house with the rest of the garden. Climbers can also be used to hide unsightly items like sheds, or to screen off the patio from the eyes of neighbours or from a view you would rather not see. The opportunities are endless. A climber can frame a window, or you can build a narrow trellis and grow climbers up it. Even a humble chain-link fence can have a climber, such as common ivy (*Hedera helix*), trained and tied to it so that it is completely covered and becomes a lush green 'wall'. If you have a wall or an unsightly feature that you want to cover rapidly, the fastest, most vigorous climber you are likely to come across is Russian vine (*Polygonum baldschuanicum*), which can cover 6m (20ft) of wall in the space of one season. However, the trouble is that once you have started it, it is difficult to get it to stop. It is deciduous, too, so you are left with bare branches in winter. But if judiciously clipped and pruned back, it quite quickly forms a thick network of stems which makes it an attractive

Left *The Japanese climbing hydrangea (*H. petiolaris*) is another vigorous grower, especially on north-facing walls. Its creamy flowers come out in June.*

around a terrace, a grape-vine traditionally makes an attractive network of leaves under which to dine out or sit. The most vigorous variety to choose is *Vitis vinifera* 'Brandt', which has foliage that colours reddish purple in the autumn and succulent black grapes.

North walls can be a problem, but fortunately there are a number of attractive climbers that will cope with them, notably *Hydrangea petiolaris*. Wisteria will also take to a north wall happily, so will the Japanese honeysuckle (*Lonicera japonica*), which will give you perfume as well.

Then there is a number of free-standing shrubs that will grow anything up to 2.5m (8ft) high and can be used in place of climbers where the backdrop is not able to take them. The best known of these is the Leyland cypress (× *Cupressocyparis leylandii*), which makes a quick-growing hedge, especially in its 'Castlewellan' form. If you want a different effect, plant it in

pairs and tie their tops together so that they bend to form a series of arches. Several of the free-standing shrubs that can be grown against a wall have attractive berries in the autumn. *Berberis darwinii*, for instance, and the somewhat smaller Oregon grape (*Mahonia aquifolium*) follow their bright yellow flowers in spring with dark purple berries; while species of *Cotoneaster*, which bear white or pink flowers in June, have rich red berries which stay on for most of the winter. The various firethorns (*Pyracantha*), too, have masses of red, orange, or yellow berries.

When buying climbers, bear in mind that container-grown plants can be put into the ground at any time of the year. Among bare-root climbers, most evergreens are planted in spring (late March or early April), while deciduous plants should be put in during their dormant period (between October and March).

Right *The 'Aurea' variety of Indian bean tree* (Catalpa bignonioides) *bears striking yellow, heart-shaped leaves.*

TREES

Trees, if you have the space for them, are a great asset in and around the patio because they provide shelter from the wind and from noise, and also help to give some degree of privacy. If you feel that an ugly building, say, or a pylon or telegraph pole at the end of the garden needs blotting from view, then a tree placed near the house will do so much better than one that is further away. But you must be careful not to shade the patio in doing so. Choose columnar trees like *Prunus* 'Amanogawa', one of the Japanese cherries, or the Dawyck beech (*Fagus sylvatica* 'Fastigiata'), both of which cast slender shadows.

Forest trees should be avoided because of their size, but in many cases smaller, fastigiate (columnar) forms of such trees have become available; they take little space and are well suited to most patios. Some of the fastigiate trees worth consideration are *Betula pendula* 'Fastigiata', an erect form of silver birch; *Carpinus betulus* 'Columnaris', a slow-growing columnar form of common hornbeam, useful for a clay soil; *Crataegus monogyna* 'Stricta', an erect form *of common hawthorn; Quercus robur* 'Fastigiata' a form of common oak; and *Ginkgo biloba* 'Fastigiata' (a columnar form of maidenhair tree).

Two weeping trees that are deservedly popular are Young's weeping birch (*Betula pendula* 'Youngii') and the purple osier (*Salix purpurea*

'Pendula'), with its purple-tinted shoot tips. Another favourite tree for town is the Indian bean-tree (*Catalpa bignonioides*), its golden form *C. b.* 'Aurea' is especially attractive and slower growing, but is not so easy to find.

The Judas tree (*Cercis siliquastrun*), with rosy clusters of pea-shaped flowers borne on the naked branches in May has great charm. The magnolias are also highly desirable trees or large shrubs; most of them are deciduous, but *M. grandiflora* is an evergreen with huge, cream,

Right *Of the various magnolias, the slow-growing* M. stellata, *which rarely exceeds 3m (10ft) in height, is the best for associating with the patio. Its fragrant flowers appear in March and April.*

sweetly fragrant goblets, and makes a superb wall shrub; *M. stellata*, though deciduous, is the one magnolia that will not ultimately outgrow the patio confines. The *Prunus* genus provides many decorative forms of cherry, peach, almond and plum, all of which adapt to town conditions, with pretty flowers in spring or early summer. Choose one of the smaller species (or a small form of one of the others): many a suburban garden suffers from an ornamental cherry or almond tree that has outgrown its site.

Trees that are grown in troughs or tubs will not achieve the same heights as those in open ground as restriction of their roots tends to have a Bonsai effect on them. It is a good idea to choose a tub with a removable side panel (many cube-shaped 'Versailles' tubs have them). This will enable you to remove and renew the soil around the roots occasionally, which is beneficial if the tree has been *in situ* for some years.

PLANTS FOR MINI-POOLS

You will need plants to aerate your pool and also some to decorate it. If possible, instal plants around the pool as well as in it; this will help to 'soften' the edges and give it a well-established look in a very short time.

A pond up to 1.5 square metres (16 sq ft) in size needs to have at least five oxygenating plants in it to keep the water sweet and clean. Permanently submerged plants such as *Elodea* and *Myriophyllum* will do this job efficiently, as will water starwort (*Callitriche stagnalis*), which also keeps algae at bay. It needs planting in heavy soil at the bottom of the pool, where it spreads to form a mat.

Apart from the familiar and well-loved water lilies (*Nymphaea*), there are a number of flowers for small ponds: two of the best are the water-violet or featherfoil (*Hottonia palustris*) and the water-soldier (*Stratiotes aloides*), which looks just like the spider plant, sending out runners with mini-plants on the end. The water soldier normally floats just under the surface of the water but comes up to bloom, when it produces white flowers in June.

Marginal plants to fringe your pond come into two categories: those that need some depth of water – about 150-450mm (6-18in) – to the shallow marginals which just want to paddle in the water to a depth of 100mm (4in) at the most. The water hawthorn (*Aponogeton distachyus*), with its starry white flowers, cotton grass with its attractive tufts, and marsh marigold (*Caltha palustris*), with its round, golden flowerheads, are all good choices.

Deep Marginal Plants	*Shallow Marginal Plants*
Aponogeton distachyus (water hawthorn)	*Alisma plantago-aquatica*
Orontium aquaticum (golden club)	*Butomus umbellatus*
Villarsia hennettii	*Iris laevigata*
	Mentha aquatica (water mint)
	Myosotis scorpioides

Above *A traditional favourite for ornamental ponds is the lovely water lily* (Nymphaea). *This is one of the* N. × laydekeri *hybrids, which are among the best for small pools.*

Left Iris laevigata *is one of the prettiest waterside plants, thriving in water up to 150mm (6in) deep.*

Above *These violet flowers identify 'Dr Mules', one of the best of the popular aubrietas.*

Right *Ericas (heaths) make attractive low-growing subjects for borders, raised beds or containers. These two are varieties of bell heather (E. cinerea).*

PERMANENT PLANTS FOR TUBS AND SMALL BEDS

With the right perennial plants installed in them, to act as a backdrop for other flowers, your tubs and flower beds can be in use all year round on the patio.

Aubrieta Low-growing, hardy evergreens that prefer a limy soil but are easy to grow. The flowers, which appear from March to June, are usually in the pink-purple colour range. *A. aurea* has leaves tinged with gold.

Buxus sempervirens 'Suffruticosus' (box) makes a good evergreen mini-hedge or can be trained into topiary. It will take shade and will grow to a maximum of 600mm (24in). 'Aurea' is a golden-leaved, slightly larger form.

Convallaria (lily-of-the-valley) Plants that like partial shade, they spread quickly and need thinning out from time to time. The waxy white, bell-like flowers appear in April or May.

Cryptomeria japonica 'Elegans Compacta' is a miniature form of the Japanese cedar with blue-green leaves that turn red-bronze in winter. It rarely reaches more than about 750mm (30in) high and wide.

Elaeagnus pungens 'Maculata' is a slow-growing evergreen with foliage boldly marked in gold. A useful mini-bush for a tub or raised bed.

Erica carnea (syn. *E. herbacea*; winter heath) One of several ericas that tolerates alkaline soils, it flowers in winter from December on and may keep in bloom until May. It rarely grows above 300mm (12in) in height.

Hebe (veronica) species also make useful evergreen mini-bushes bearing white flowers in summer. *H.* 'Autumn Glory' has purplish green leaves, *H.* 'Pagei' has light green leaves and is the smallest version, reaching about 300mm (12in).

Hedera (ivy) makes a marvellous evergreen trailer, climber or ground cover plant in tubs and raised beds. Common ivy (*H. helix*) comes in many variegated forms too, notably 'Goldheart', which has small dark leaves with gold centres, and 'Glacier', with leaves variegated with silver grey, edged with white. *Juniperus communis* 'Compressa' is a dwarf juniper with attractive grey-green foliage which grows, very slowly, seldom more than 750mm (30in) high.

Lavandula angustifolia 'Munstead' A dwarf version of the traditional lavender which can be clipped to make an attractive edging or left as a small bush.

Lonicera nitida 'Baggesen's Gold' One of the evergreen honeysuckles, this useful plant has tiny golden leaves and can be clipped into topiary shapes if you wish.

Lysimachia nummularia (creeping jenny) A useful ground-covering plant which produces

Left *The 'Compressa' variety of common juniper* (Juniperus communis) *is no more than 600mm (2ft) high, and its columnar shape makes it an ideal subject for patio containers.*

Above *The lesser periwinkle* (Vinca minor) *makes a fine ground-cover plant. Its flowers bloom at intervals from spring to mid-autumn.*

yellow cup-shaped flowers in June and July. *Rosa* Miniature roses come now in many different forms – there are even climbing/trailing miniatures, none of which reach more than about 450mm (18in) high. If you plant these make sure that they are in a sunny position and that they have rich soil to grow in.

Saxifraga × urbium (London pride) Another useful inhabitant for a tub, this member of the saxifrage family prefers shade and produces masses of small pink flowers in early summer.

Senecio cineraria. Not always hardy in this country, it survives some winters in a sheltered spot and is invaluable for setting off colourful flowers late on. Its leaves, covered with woolly hairs, have an attractive silvery look and are deeply indented. It reaches a height of about 600mm (24in).

Vinca minor (lesser periwinkle) makes useful evergreen ground-cover for larger tubs and raised beds. It will also trail over the sides of containers. It has pretty blue cup-shaped flowers in summer and can be relied upon to spread to about 450mm (18in). Varieties are avaialble, some with white or purple flowers; some with variegated foliage.

SHRUBS FOR TUBS

Always be generous with the depth of a container for a shrub or small tree if it is to stay there for any length of time. The plants will be less likely to dry out and will thrive given plenty of room. Remember that shrubs in tubs under the shade of trees or beside walls may not get their full share of rain, so check them and water them regularly.

Azaleas (Rhododendron) come in both evergreen and deciduous hybrids. Superb deciduous forms include the Ghent, Mollis and Knaphill hybrids; evergreens include the Kaempferi, Kurume and Vuyk groups. *Camellia × williamsii* 'Donation' has glossy evergreen foliage and large soft pink flowers resembling open roses. The Japanese quince *(Chaenomeles × superba)* makes a fine wall shrub. Several excellent varieties are available with spring flowers in shades of red, pink or white. Lawson's cypress *(Chamaecyparis lawsoniana)* makes a good tub conifer if you choose the right (slow-growing) cultivar. Names to look out for include 'Ellwood's Gold', with grey-blue foliage with yellow shoot-tips; and 'Minima Aurea', pyramid-shaped, which has branches edged with gold, and is excellent for a small container.

Deutzia × elegantissima, a most elegant hybrid, has scented, rose-tinted white flowers on arching branches; look for variety 'Rosealind'. *Elaeagnus pungens* 'Maculata', a dense, spreading evergreen, with silvery flowers in autumn, has variegated evergreen foliage splashed with yellow. *Escallonia* 'Donard Radiance' is a pretty shrub with attractive pink flowers in early summer and large, glossy leaves.

One of the finest of the camellias, the 'Donation' variety of C. × williamsii will grow to a height of 2.5m (8¼ft), with flowers as much as 100mm (4in) across.

Above *The Hortensia hydrangeas bear flower-heads that are more than 150mm (6in) in diameter.*

Left *The 'Rosealind' variety of* Deutzia × elegantissima *grows up to 1.5m (5ft) high and wide.*

Above *Hybrids of the pretty mock orange* (Philadelphus) *grow to 2m (6½ft); the delightfully fragrant flowers come out in June and July.*

Fuchsia are well-known patio plants, but unless you pick the hardy varieties the tub will have to overwinter indoors. Outdoor varieties include 'Alice Hoffman', Corallina', 'Mrs Popple', 'Tennessee Waltz'; 'Tom Thumb' is a good miniature. *Hydrangea macrophylla* produces large panicles of paper-like pink, blue or white flowers. Acid soil in the tub produces blue flowers; chalky soil produces pink ones. Some dwarf forms are available. The mock-orange (*Philadelphus*) is a pleasant shrub to have near the house; the white flowers are scented like orange-blossom. Good hybrids include 'Beau-clerk' (single flowers), 'Belle Etoile' (single), and 'Manteau d'Hermine' (double).

The modern compact rhododendron hybrids are fully hardy and most are not more than 1.2m (4ft) high and wide. Examples include 'Bluebird' (violet-blue flowers), 'Scarlet Wonder' (scarlet). Sweet-scented, grey-foliaged rosemary (*Rosmarinus officinalis*) is a useful evergreen to have around the patio, especially if you have installed a barbecue. The slow-growing yew (*Taxus baccata*) takes well to topiary – a bird, bear or other small beast would make an amusing decoration for the patio.

Right *Bear's-breech* (Acanthus) *are striking perennials that flower in July-August.*

FLOWERS AND FOLIAGE FOR TUBS AND RAISED BEDS

Plants which give colour just where it is wanted are a valuable asset around the patio. So are those with leaves of an interesting shape or texture which act as a foil to summer bedding flowers and, in most cases, provide some interest all year round.

Acanthus (bear's breech) are attractive foliage plants with tall spikes of flowers varying from lavender to white. The dwarf varieties of yarrow (*Achillea*) are good for rockeries or containers. *A. chrysocoma* has woolly grey-green leaves and yellow flowers; *A. clavenae* has white daisy-like blooms. *Adonis amurensis* is a pretty, low-growing plant with bright yellow flowers in February-March and matt-green, fern-like foliage; it prefers a partially shaded situation and is good to underplant among taller plants.

Below *Largest of the common decorative onion plants,* Allium giganteum *grows up to 1.2m (4ft) high and blooms in June.*

Aethionema pulchellum is a compact plant with attractive dark pink flowers. Basically a rockery plant, it grows well in tubs and window-boxes. African lilies (*Agapanthus*) are showy specimen plants for tubs and small borders; they can also be grown in a box alongside a terrace. Choose the hardy *A. inapertus*, which has deep violet-blue flowers. *Agave* makes a marvellous foliage plant, especially if you want a tropical look in a tub or a border. *A. americana* 'Marginata' (syn. 'Variegata') has narrow sword-like leaves edged with gold; *A. victoriae-reginae* forms a pompon head like a cactus. They are not completely hardy and are best brought indoors during the winter.

Lady's mantle (*Alchemilla*) is another handsome foliage plant that is often used for flower arrangements and which looks good in a tub. *A. mollis* has star-shaped yellow-green flowers and will self-seed. *Allium giganteum* is a decorative form of onion which makes a good feature plant in a small bed. It forms deep lilac flower heads which can be dried for decoration indoors. The Peruvian lily (*Alstroemeria*) is a striking plant with flowers somewhere between those of orchids and gladioli in appearance. *A. aurantiaca* has flowers ranging from yellow to scarlet.

Alyssum is a reliable carpeting plant for tubs, dry-stone walls and rockeries. *A. argenteum* has bright yellow flowers; *A. maritimum* (strictly *Lobularia maritima*) has white or lilac flowers and is low-growing. The scarlet pimpernel

Left *On a fully paved patio a long, low trough can be planted up like a mixed border.*

Below *The* Agave victoriae-reginae, *one of the smaller of its kind, makes a fine specimen plant for the patio.*

(*Anagallis arvensis*) is a pretty, prostrate plant with small red flowers. It is an annual, but it will generally self-seed for the next year. *A. arvensis* 'Caerulea' is a form with dark blue flowers. The Japanese windflower (*Anemone* × *hybrida*) is an attractive large-flowered anemone which blooms from August to October. The variety 'Queen Charlotte' has attractive semi-double pink flowers.

There are many forms of chamomile (*Anthemis*), ranging from the carpeting (non-flowering) *Anthemis nobilis* 'Treneague' to the yellow or ox-eye chamomile (*A. tinctoria*). One of the most decorative varieties is *A. sancti-johannis*, with bright orange flowers. The columbine (*Aquilegia*) makes delicate, attractive flowers to grow in a small space. *A. longissima* has pretty yellow flowers on slender stems; *A. bertolonii* is a small Alpine version that looks, at a distance, rather like edelweiss; *A. vulgaris*, which comes in many colours, is the best-known columbine.

The thrifts (*Armeria*) are useful plants to edge a tub or go between paving stones. They produce hummocks of spiky grass-like leaves and pink flower heads. There are several different species, ranging from *A. caespitosa*, which grows only 50-75mm (2-3in) high, to *A. maritima* which can reach 300mm (12in). *Artemisia* are grown for their silvery white leaves; they are useful plants to mix with colourful annual flowers. *A. stelleriana* (dusty miller) has leaves that are almost white, and yellow flowers; *A. gnaphalodes* has woolly white leaves. *Asperula suberosa* is a small semi-training plant (a relative of sweet woodruff) that has a profusion of pretty pink flowers and white, hairy leaves.

Aster is a large genus, best known for the Michaelmas daisies. Asters have flowers in purples, blues, reds, and pinks. The smallest is *A. alpinus*, which has purple-blue flowers with orange-yellow centres. If growing true Michaelmas daisies (such as *A. novi-belgii*), pick a dwarf variety such as 'Audrey', 'Lady in Blue', or 'Professor Kippenburg'.

Begonias are a great standby for tubs, hanging baskets, and window-boxes. The fibrous-rooted *B. semperflorens* has small flowers in red, pink, or white, and leaves ranging from glossy green to bronze-purple. The tuberous-rooted begonias of the Pendula group (*B. × tuberhybrida*) make good trailers for hanging baskets; examples include 'Dawn' (yellow), 'Golden Shower', 'Lou Anne' (pink), and 'Red Cascade' (scarlet).

The pot marigold (*Calendula officinalis*) is the true marigold, with its double daisy-like flowers in bright orange (though you can also get versions with creamy, apricot, even pink flowers) and growing to a height of 500mm (20in) or more. 'Kelmscott Giant Orange' is a good one to choose; 'Pacific Beauty' will give you a mixture of colours. Their long flowering season lasts from the last days of spring to the first frosts of autumn.

Callirhoes are basically rock-garden plants; they are dwarf trailers with simple bowl-shaped, mauve-red flowers produced in mid-summer. *C. involucrata* is a good version to choose. Good dwarf annuals are available in bedding strains of the China aster (*Callistephus chinensis*). Of slightly larger forms, Lilliput Mixed, with flowers ranging from white to crimson, is particularly suitable for small tubs; it blooms from mid-summer to early autumn.

Indian shot (*Canna × generalis*) bears showy, tropical-looking flowers and makes a good specimen in tubs. Good cultivars are 'Orange Perfection' and 'President', which has bright scarlet flowers. Chionodoxas are good spring-flowering bulbs to go under permanent plantings in a tub, Glory-of-the-snow (*C. luciliae*) has light blue flowers with white centres. *C. sardensis* has deeper-blue flowers.

Chrysanthemums contribute a huge range of very reliable flowers for tubs and boxes. Look for the attractive alpine species, *C. alpinum*, for very-small-scale planting; it rarely grows taller than 150mm (6in). It has white daisy-like flowers in July and August. *C. carinatum*, a North African annual, is much taller – up to 600mm (24in) – and has very colourful flowers over a longer season.

The hardy outdoor forms of the cyclamen, a very popular plant, are smaller and much more delicate-looking than indoor types. One of the best is *C. coum*, with pink flowers in winter.

Dahlias are available in a vast variety, ranging from those with pompon heads to simple versions almost like huge daisies. For small areas choose the dwarf varieties of bedding dahlias: a good example is 'Early Bird', which has semi-double flowers in pink, yellow, orange, and deep red. Pinks and carnations (*Dianthus*) are real cottage-garden flowers, including sweet william (*D. barbatus*). *D. alpinus*, which is basically a rock-garden plant, is useful if space is limited. Miniature versions of the so-called Modern pinks include 'Bombardier', which has red flowers, and 'Fay', which has mauve flowers.

Left *Glory-of-the-snow* (Chionodoxa) *makes a good underplanting bulb for tubs; its flowers come out in March to late April.*

Below, left '*Yellow Spiky*' *is typical of the cactus group of dahlias, flowering from August to mid-autumn.*

Plants for sheltered spots

Agapanthus
Agave americana
Amaryllis belladonna
Ballota pseudodictamnus
Berberidopsis
Buddleia fallowiana
Callistemon
Calocephalus
Camellia sasanqua
Campsis
Centaurea gymnocarpa
Chrysanthemum ptarmacaefolium
Cistus
Clerodendron
Clianthus
Crinum
Convolvulus cneorum
Dimorphotheca
Gazania
Hebe hybrids
Helichrysum petiolatum
Indigofera
Jasminum officinalis
Lapageria
Mesembryanthemum
Mutisia
Nerine
Nerium oleander
Passiflora caerulea
Piptanthus
Senecio cineraria
Sparaxis
Teucrium fruticans
Tigridia
Tropaeolum tuberosum
Yucca

Above *The annual and perennial forms of sea lavender* (Limonium) *flower in late summer to early autumn; the annuals, especially varieties of* L. sinuatum, *make good everlasting flowers.*

Above *Leopard's banes (this one is* Doronicum plantagineum) *grow to about 600mm (2ft) and flower in June.*

Leopard's banes (*Doronicum*) are daisy-like flowers which bloom early and, if dead-headed regularly, will often produce a second flush in the autumn. *D. columnae* has single golden yellow flowers. Fleabane (*Erigeron*) has daisy-like flowerheads in pinks, blues, and yellows. *E aureus* is typical and bears yellow flowers about 25mm (1in) across in June and July. The Californian poppy (*Eschscholzia californica*) produces masses of orange or yellow flowers. A good dwarf species is *E. caespitosa*.

Crane's-bills (*Geranium*) are true geraniums – not to be confused with pelargoniums – and they too make good plants for a tub. They have pretty pink, white or blue flowers and lacy leaves. *G. dalmaticum* is an almost alpine species that makes a broad cushion of light pink flowers. Avens (*Geum*) are good in display beds or, in the case of alpine varieties, in small window-boxes and hanging baskets. *G. montanum* and *G. reptans* are excellent dwarf versions, their yellow flowers followed by interesting silvery seed heads.

Godetias are hardy annuals with double or single flowers. *G. grandiflora* is one of the most attractive, with rose-purple blooms; its cultivar 'Azalea-flowered Mixed' has frilled petals. St John's worts (*Hypericum*) are useful yellow flowers for a raised bed. Rose-of-Sharon (*H. calycinum*) is the most commonly planted species, but *H. patulum* 'Hidcote' is a more attractive plant if you have the space for it. St John's worts give berries and coloured foliage in the autumn. Candytufts (*Iberis*) are good plants for town gardens since they stand up well to atmospheric pollution. *I. amara* has pink-carmine flowers.

Statice, or sea lavenders (*Limonium*), make delightful, ideal 'everlasting' flowers when they have done their duty in summer. Attractive Mediterranean annuals, they come in many different colours. *L. sinuatum* and its cultivars are best if you want the dried flowers. Toadflaxes (*Linaria alpina*) make pretty plants to put among paving stones. They have purple snapdragon-like flowers.

Bells of Ireland (*Moluccella laevis*) is an unusual plant with curious green flowers that make an interesting effect if put in a tub. It looks good if mixed with white flowers; and the flower-heads can be dried for winter decoration. *Nemesia strumosa* is a useful half-hardy plant for a mixed display. Choose the cultivar 'Carnival Mixed', a dwarf version with flowers in various vivid colours. Poppies *(Papaver)* are excellent in raised beds and tubs, especially when mixed with plants with silvery foliage. If you are worried about height, choose the alpine poppy *(P. alpinum)*, which is available with flowers of white, yellow, red, and orange. The Iceland poppy *(P. nudicaule)* has flowers with petals like tissue paper and is particularly attractive.

Phlox drummondii is an annual with flowers of pink, purple, lavender, red, and white. *Salvia splendens* makes a good standby if you need a splash of colour. Its cultivar 'Blaze of Fire' has particularly brilliant flowers of bright scarlet. Lamb's tongue *(Stachys lanata)* is grown for its distinctive woolly foliage, which makes a good foil to colourful bedding plants. Its spikes of purple blooms open in midsummer. Speedwell *(Veronica)* includes a group of alpines useful as ground-cover plants, ranging from *V. cinerea*, with pink flowers, to the carpet-like bright-blue-flowered *V. filiformis*.

Left *Bells-of-Ireland* (Moluccella laevis) *has intriguing green flowers. Growing to a height of 600mm (2ft), it makes a good companion for white-flowered plants.*

Below *By contrast, the brilliant oriental poppy* (Papaver orientale), *a perennial, often looks best with foliage plants for company. It flowers in May-June.*

BEDDING PLANTS FOR BOXES, BASKETS & TUBS

Colour is what you want when choosing display plants for boxes and hanging baskets. Never be afraid to experiment: unusual combinations like hot oranges, reds and yellows can look quite spectacular; so can the cool colours, the blues mixed with green. Or, for a very sophisticated look, try a one-tone arrangement like white. Switch your colour schemes around from year to year to vary the look of your patio; co-ordinate coloured boxes to match your living-room curtains to add to the effect of an outdoor room.

Ageratum houstonianum is a fluffy blue, pink or white flower from Mexico. 'Blue Chip' and 'Fairy Pink' are long-flowering varieties. *Alyssum* perennials make good, compact flowers in almost all colours of the rainbow. Cut back well after flowering to keep them in shape. (The alyssum annuals are now classified under *Lobularia*.)

Snapdragons (*Antirrhinum*), notably the dwarf bedding varieties, are available in many colours. Planted out in May they will produce a succession of blooms throughout summer and into autumn. Another reliable, long-flowering

Two invaluable small-flowered trailers for hanging baskets are alyssums (here in white but available in pinks and purples) and lobelias (blue here but also common in light blue, red and mixtures).

Left *Another favourite container plant is the fibrous-rooted begonia* (B. semperflorens), *available in reds, pinks and whites. It flowers from June to October.*

Below *The slipper-flower* (Calceolaria integrifolia) *blooms from July to September. Slightly tender, it needs a sunny, sheltered spot.*

favourite *Begonia semperflorens* – the fibrous-rooted type – comes in many colours, from white through cream to deep reds and pinks, with leaves that are green or bronze.

Slipper-flowers (*Calceolaria*), often grown as indoor plants, have distinctive spotted, pouch-shaped flowers in reds and yellows. They can be planted out after the last frosts and will go on through the summer. The China aster (*Callistephus chinensis*) has many cultivars with flowers that vary from those looking like a daisy to complicated chrysanthemum-like blooms in pinks, blues, and white.

Star-of-Bethlehem (*Campanula isophylla*), a relative of the Canterbury bell, can be grown in a container in a warm, sheltered position, where it rewards you with heart-shaped leaves and starry, bell-like flowers over a long period from late spring to autumn.

The dwarf varieties of cockscomb (*Celosia argentea*) are best for patio plantings. Forms such as 'Golden Feather', 'Fiery Feather', 'Lilliput' Mixed', or 'Jewel Box' have plume-like flowers in reds and yellows and bloom throughout summer. Cornflowers (*Centaurea*) come in other shades than cornflower blue – deep scarlet, for instance. Cornflowers are best grown *in situ* from seed. Choose *C. imperialis* for good compact patio plants. A compact form of another traditional favourite is the Siberian wallflower (*Cheiranthus* × *allionii*). Two good varieties are 'Golden Queen' and 'Orange Queen'.

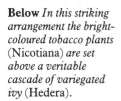

Right *Busy-lizzie* (Impatiens wallerana) *is one of the best and longest-flowering of the bedding plants, a particular favourite for hanging baskets. Many colours are available; this vermilion form is* 'Blitz'.

Below *In this striking arrangement the bright-coloured tobacco plants* (Nicotiana) *are set above a veritable cascade of variegated ivy* (Hedera).

Marguerite, or Paris daisy (*Chrysanthemum frutescens*), is a bushy perennial which produces abundant white daisies with yellow centres. An ideal plant to train as a flowering standard in an ornamental pot, if given plenty of sunlight it will bloom from spring to autumn.

Cinerarias (strictly *Senecio* species) are very popular bedding plants for window-boxes, pro-ducing masses of close-packed flowers in the spring. *Senecio cruentus* (syn. *Cineraria cruenta*) 'Gem Mixed' is a good variety, with flowers (some bicoloured) in pink, red, lilac and purple. Stocks (*Matthiola*) are cottage-garden flowers that thrive in boxes and baskets. The night-scented stock (*M. bicornis*), bears perfumed lavender flowers; other varieties come in pinks, blues and white. Plant it in pots or baskets near house windows to enjoy its lovely evening fragrance.

The Livingstone daisy (*Mesembryanthemum criniflorum*, syn. *Dorotheanthus bellidiformis*) is a tiny succulent plant that likes plenty of sun, and produces rich pink and orange flowers. *Nemesia strumosa*, a half-hardy annual, makes compact plants with large flowers in a variety of colours: 'Suttons Mixed' is in red-orange tones; 'Blue Gem' has blue flowers. Tobacco plants (*Nicotiana*) are grown as much for their fragrance as for their looks. Flowers come in white, sharp yellow-green, and reds.

Pelargoniums are great window-box and hanging-basket standbys. Choose the zonal varieties for height and the ivy-leaved varieties for climbers or trailers. Look out for scented-leaved varieties, too: their flowers are unremarkable, but the fine-toothed leaves are fragrant and attractive.

The petunia (*Petunia × hybrida*) is one of the showiest window-box plants with white, pink, red or blue flowers. It can be had in standard, dwarf, or trailing varieties and is very good for hanging baskets as well as for boxes. It blooms throughout the summer and on into September. The polyanthus, or polyantha primroses (*Primula*), are hardy perennials available in a variety of delightful colours that will light up the patio in late spring. They can be left as permanent occupants of pots and tubs provided that they are divided from time to time after flowering.

Salvia species are colourful plants with bright red spike-like flowers that are good for formal boxes. Mother-of-thousands (*Saxifraga stolonifera*, syn *S. sarmentosa*), often grown as a houseplant, can also be grown out of doors in summer. It is liked for its colourful leaves – green tinged with pink and silver, with plantlets on runners.

Among several types of marigold, choose the French form (*Tagetes patula*) if you want a low-growing plant; the African variety (*T. erecta*) is somewhat taller. Delicately scented, the African marigold has pompon blooms in pale yellows through to red; the French marigold has single or double flowers in the same colours.

Verbena peruviana, a low-growing perennial that needs shelter in the winter, bears brilliant scarlet, star-shaped flowers in great profusion in summer. Heartsease (*Viola tricolor*) is a pretty low-grower which comes in a wide variety of colours and blooms in mid-summer. *Zinnia elegans* resembles a chrysanthemum; the compact cultivar 'Lilliput', about 250mm (10in) tall, is the best form for boxes and baskets. Even smaller is 'Thumbelina', which rarely exceeds 150mm (6in). Both varieties have multi-coloured flowers that bloom from June to September.

Two other plants for a long-flowering season: petunias (here mainly reds, purple, lilac and white) and pelargoniums (pink, at top).

CHECKLIST OF PERMANENT PLANT RESIDENTS

Name	Description	Height/spread*	Flowering period	Soil and site	Remarks
Arbutus unedo (strawberry tree)	An attractive evergreen tree with red pitcher-shaped flowers and strawberry-like fruits at the same time.	H:4.5m (15ft) S:3m (10ft)	Oct	Provide a neutral soil in a sheltered, sunny position	Plant in Oct. or in March, April or May. Young plants may need protection from cold winds
Aucuba japonica	A good shrub for a polluted atmosphere, and for planting in shade. The type has large green leaves, but there is an attractive variegated form, *A. j.* 'Variegata'. The female plants bear red berries	H:1.8m (6ft) S:1.5m (5ft)	March-April	Any good garden soil is suitable, in a shady or semi-shaded position. Can be planted safely in coastal areas	For a good crop of berries, plant one male to three or four female plants
Berberis darwinii (Darwin's barberry)	A first-class evergreen shrub with small shining green leaves and a mass of bright orange-yellow flowers. Attractive bluish-purple berries appear later	H:2.1m (7ft) S:2.1m (7ft)	April-May	Any good soil suits this plant, in sun or light shade	Plant Sept. and Oct. or March and April. No pruning is required, but old shoots can be cut back to ground level
B. × stenophylla (barberry)	An evergreen shrub, ideal as a specimen on its own or as a hedge. It produces cascades of orange-yellow flowers	H:3m (10ft) S:3m (10ft)	May	Ordinary soil in sun or light shade	Plant in Sept. and Oct. or March and April. Pruning consists only of cutting out dead wood and trimming to shape
B. thunbergii (Thunberg's barberry)	A valuable leaf-shedding shrub, producing bright red fruit and foliage in autumn. Some forms have reddish-purple foliage all summer	H:1.5m (5ft) S:1.5m (5ft)	May	Ordinary soil in a sunny position	Little pruning is required other than trimming to shape
Buddleia davidii (butterfly bush)	The large, tapering flower heads – mainly shades of blue or purple, but sometimes white – are very attractive to butterflies. A good shrub	H:2.1m (7ft) S:2.1m (7ft)	July-Aug	Provide good soil in full sun. Will tolerate a limy soil	Plant Oct and Nov or March and April. To prune, cut back the previous season's growth to within 75mm (3in) of old wood
Buxus sempervirens (box)	A traditional hedging plant with small green leaves	H:3m+ (10ft+) S:1.8m+ (6ft+)	–	Any good garden soil is suitable, in sun or light shade	Clip to shape as required, in spring and late summer. Plant autumn or spring
Calluna vulgaris (Scottish heather, ling)	There are many cultivars of this popular plant, from carpeters of only 50mm (2in) such as 'Golden Carpet' to tall kinds 900mm (3ft) high. Most have olive-green foliage, while others have golden, bronze or silver hues. The flowers are white, pink, purple and red	H:50-900mm (2-36in) S:75-900mm (3-36in)	Aug-Nov	These plants are tolerant of salt-laden spray and will even survive moderate atmospheric pollution. Give them a sunny site and lime-free soil	Lightly trim to shape and remove dead heads after flowering season is over
Camellia japonica	An evergreen shrub with beautiful peony-like flowers, chiefly in shades of red and pink, but also white.	H:1.8m (6ft) S:1.8m (6ft)	March-April	Choose a sheltered position, out of the direct rays of early-morning sun. A peaty, acid soil is essential	Plant in Sept and Oct or March and April. Keep young plants moist. Mulch deeply with peat
Chaenomeles speciosa (flowering quince)	A spectacular shrub when trained against a wall. The flowers are chiefly red, pink, or white. The fruits are edible and used in preserves.	H:1.8m (6ft) S:1.8m (6ft)	March-May	Although this plant will grow on an east or north wall, it does best in a sunny position. Ordinary soil	If grown as a bush, little pruning is required – just trim to shape. If a wall shrub, cut back previous season's growth in May to two or three buds
Chamaecyparis lawsoniana (Lawson cypress)	The species is a large conical conifer with broad fan-like sprays of foliage, but there are many cultivars	H:6m+ (20ft+) S:1.8m+ (6ft+)	–	Will thrive on most soils, including those in exposed sites and shady aspect	Plant in Oct on light soil, in March or April on cold, exposed sites or heavy ground.

Chimonanthus praecox (syn. *C. fragrans*; winter sweet)	An excellent wall shrub for winter bloom. The yellow, fragrant flowers are borne on bare twigs	H:2.4m (8ft) S:2.4m (8ft)	Dec-Jan	An excellent plant for chalk, but will succeed on any well-drained soil	Plant against a south- or west-facing wall in a sheltered position. Plants do not flower well until established for a few years
Cistus (sun rose)	An evergreen shrub with flowers that resemble single roses, usually white with blotches, but may be pinkish depending on species	H:0.6-2.4m (2-8ft) S:0.6-2.4m (2-8ft)	June-July	Good plants for hot, dry sites, and will grow happily on chalk. Also wind-tolerant and suitable for coastal areas	These plants resent root disturbance, so plant pot-grown specimens in spring. Keep the plants watered at first. Some species are not very tolerant of severe frosts
Clematis (large-flowered hybrids)	There are many cultivars of this popular climber, with flowers in all shades of blue, pink, purple, red and white. Some are attractively striped or shaded	H:3.5m (12ft)	May-June and Sept-Oct	A loamy soil containing lime is preferred. The roots should be in shade, but the top growth in sun	Clematis respond to an annual mulch of well-rotted compost or manure, and plenty of water throughout summer
C. montana	An extremely vigorous small-flowered clematis, white in the type, pink in some cultivars	H: up to 9m (30ft)	May	As large-flowered type	Immediately after flowering cut out all shoots that have flowered
C. tangutica	A vigorous small-flowered species with yellow lantern-like flowers, and decorative silky seed-heads	H:4.5m (15ft)	June-Oct	As large-flowered type	During Feb or March, cut back all shoots to a strong pair of buds 900mm (3ft) or less above the ground
***Cotoneaster conspicuus* 'Decorus'**	An evergreen shrub suitable for the rock garden or small border, where its prostrate habit is useful. Miniature hawthorn flowers are followed by red berries	H:300mm (1ft) S:600mm (2ft)	May-July	Almost any soil in sun or semi-shade will suit	Plant in Oct or in March and April. Regular pruning is not required, but if desired trim back in spring
C. horizontalis (fish-bone cotoneaster)	A low-growing shrub for covering banks, or for positioning against a wall. The branches have a herring-bone-like appearance, in autumn covered with red berries	H:600mm (2ft) S:1.8m (6ft)	June	Any good soil in sun or partial shade	A trouble-free plant requiring no special attention other than trimming to shape
***C. × hybridus* 'Pendulus'**	An ideal small evergreen weeping tree for the restricted garden. Large red berries are produced in autumn	H:2.4m (8ft) S:1.8m (6ft)	June	A sunny position and any reasonable soil will suit this plant	Plant in Oct or in March or April
Cytisus battandieri (pineapple broom)	A distinctive shrub of upright, somewhat tree-like habit for a south or west wall. The cone-shaped clusters of yellow flowers have a scent like that of pineapple	H:3m (10ft) S:2.4m (8ft)	July	A well-drained soil in a sunny position is essential. Plant against a sunny wall	The plant is not hardy in cold districts. Plant in Sept or Oct, or in April
C. × kewensis	An outstanding shrub of semi-prostrate habit with masses of creamy flowers	H:300mm (1ft) S:1.2m (4ft)	May	A deep, neutral soil, well-drained and in full sun is best	Plant from pots in September or March. Trim back the shoots after flowering
C. scoparius (broom)	A familiar shrub with yellow pea-like flowers. There are cultivars with red, brownish or cream flowers	H:1.8m (6ft) S:1.8m (6ft)	May	Best on a slightly acid soil, in full sun	Plant from pots, in Sept and Oct or in March and April. After flowering, cut off most of previous season's growth
Daboecia cantabrica (Irish heath)	A heather-like plant with rosy-purple, white, pink or purple bells	H:600mm (2ft) S:600mm (2ft)	May-Oct	A peaty, acid soil in full sun or partial shade is necessary	Provide sheltered site in exposed areas. Cut off dead flowers in spring

PLANTS FOR THE PATIO

CHECKLIST OF PERMANENT PLANT RESIDENTS

Name	Description	Height/spread*	Flowering period	Soil and site	Remarks
Daphne mezereum (mezereon)	An outstandingly beautiful early-flowering shrub with fragrant purple-red blooms. A white cultivar is also available: *D. m.* 'Alba'	H:1.2m (4ft) S:900mm (3ft)	Feb-March	Any good, well-drained soil in sun or partial shade is suitable	Plant in Sept or March
Elaeagnus pungens 'Maculata' (wood olive)	A variegated evergreen shrub with green leaves attractively splashed deep yellow. The flowers are fragrant	H:2.4m (8ft) S:2.4m (8ft)	Oct-Nov	Will thrive on any fertile soil other than chalk. Plant in sun or semi-shade	A trouble-free plant. Prune to shape as necessary
Erica carnea (syn. *E. herbacea;* heath)	A valuable winter-flowering dwarf shrub, with many cultivars in all shades of pink and purple, as well as white.	H:150-300mm (6-12in) S:600mm (2ft)	Dec-April	Although lime-tolerant, avoid shallow chalky soil. Plant in sun or semi-shade	After flowering, remove dead heads with shears
Forsythia × intermedia (golden bell bush)	One of our most popular spring-flowering shrubs, with long arching sprays of yellow, bell-shaped flowers	H:2.4m (8ft) S:2.4m (8ft)	April-May	Plant in any good soil, in sun or partial shade	Prune immediately after flowering, removing old and damaged wood and shortening vigorous flowered shoots
Genista hispanica (Spanish gorse)	A plant related to brooms, covered in late spring with masses of yellow flowers. Forms a compact, prickly mound	H:600mm (2ft) S:1.5m (5ft)	May-June	Will succeed in acid or neutral soil, but is also tolerant of lime. Provide a hot, sunny site	A trouble-free plant requiring no regular attention
Hedera colchica (Persian ivy)	A vigorous climber with large heart-shaped leaves. Variegated forms best	H:6m (20ft)	Sept-Oct	Will thrive in almost any soil or situation. Self-clinging	Trim back stray shoots, to control shape
H. helix (common ivy)	There are cultivars with a wide variety of leaf shapes and variegations	H:12m (40ft)	Sept-Oct	Suitable for any soil or situation. Self-clinging	Cut out stray shoots to keep under control
Hydrangea petiolaris (climbing hydrangea)	A vigorous self-clinging climber with heart-shaped leaves and large heads of white flowers	H:9m (30ft)	June	Prefers a moist soil. Ideal for a shady wall (height will be more than stated if growing in a tree, less on a wall)	Plant in Oct and Nov or March and April
H. paniculata 'Grandiflora'	Large spikes of creamy-white flowers, like a large white lilac. A showy shrub	H:4m (13ft) S:3m (10ft)	July-Aug	Provide a moisture-retentive soil well enriched with organic matter	Plant in Oct and Nov or March and April.
Hypericum patulum 'Hidcote' (St John's wort)	An impressive shrub with numerous large golden-yellow saucer-shaped flowers. Well worth growing	H:1.5m (5ft) S:1.2m (4ft)	July-Sept	Will thrive in a well-drained soil, and be happy in full sun or semi-shade	Each March cut back the previous year's growth to within a few inches of old wood
Ilex aquifolium 'Aureo-marginata' (holly)	An attractive holly with yellow-margined leaves. Forms a nice hedge or a specimen tree	H:4.5m (15ft) S:2.4m (8ft)	May-June	Will grow on most soils, in sun or shade. Tolerant of atmospheric pollution and coastal planting	Plant in Oct or March. Specimen trees require no pruning; clip hedges to shape in Aug
Jasminum nudiflorum (winter jasmine)	An attractive wall shrub with beautiful small yellow flowers in winter	H:3m (10ft)	Nov-March	Will grow happily in most soils	After flowering, cut back flowered growths to 50-75mm (2-3in) of their base
Kerria japonica (jew's mallow)	Attractive yellow flowers (double in the cultivar 'Pleniflora') on slender arching green branches	H:1.8m (6ft) S:1.8m (6ft)	April-May	Will grow in any ordinary garden soil; best planted against a wall. Sun or semi-shade	Shoots that have flowered should be cut back to strong growth
Lonicera japonica 'Aureoreticulata' (Japanese honeysuckle)	A rampant semi-evergreen climber with small leaves conspicuously reticulated with gold	H:4.5m (15ft)	June-Aug	Best on a south, east or west-facing wall. Will be happy in most soils	Plant during April or May. Thin out shoots that become overcrowded

L. nitida (shrubby honeysuckle)	A small-leaved bushy plant often used for hedges, but can be used as a free-standing specimen – especially the golden cultivar 'Baggessen's Gold'. Evergreen	H:1.5m (5ft) S:1.5m (5ft)	–	Will thrive in any normal garden soil, in sun or shade	No regular pruning required unless grown as a hedge
L. periclymenum '**Serotina**' (late Dutch honeysuckle)	A vigorous climber with strongly-scented reddish-purple and yellow flowers	H:4.5m (15ft)	Aug-Sept	Best in good loam, in a position of semi-shade	Plant in spring. Trim only to keep in shape
Mahonia aquifolium (Oregon grape)	A small evergreen shrub with large holly-shaped leaves, which take on a purple tinge in autumn. Yellow flowers are followed by black berries in summer	H:900mm (3ft) S:900mm (3ft)	Feb-April	Mahonias will grow in most types of soil, including chalk. Will grow happily in shade	Plant in Sept and Oct or April and May
Parthenocissus quinquefolia (Virginia creeper)	A climber noteworthy for its deeply cut, five-lobed leaves, which turn orange and scarlet in autumn. Self-clinging	H:15m+ (50ft+)	–	These plants prefer a good loam, with unrestricted root-run. Sun or semi-shade	Remove unwanted or straggly growth in late summer
Polygonum baldschuanicum (Russian vine)	One of the most vigorous climbing shrubs, with masses of white flowers. Ideal for hiding unsightly objects	H:6m+ (20ft+)	July-Oct	Any soil will suit this plant, including chalk	Plant in spring, using pot-grown specimens. The only routine care is trimming to control growth
Prunus (ornamental fruit trees)	The *Prunus* provide many fine garden trees, the ornamental almonds, peaches and Japanese cherries being among the best	H:6-7.5m (20-25ft) S:6-7.5m (20-25ft)	April	A well-drained, lime-free soil is best	Plant in Aug, Sept or March. Grown as a shrub, height will be 3-4.5m (10-15ft).
Pyracantha (firethorn)	A highly desirable shrub to grow against a wall, or on its own. Berries are the outstanding feature, usually orange-red	H:3m (10ft) S:3m (10ft)	May-June	Will grow in any fertile soil, and is tolerant of exposure. Sun or semi-shade	Wall specimens can be lightly trimmed back in July
Rhododendron	A large group of shrubs, most hardy, for acid soil. Flowers in red, pink, yellow and white, often beautifully marked. Evergreen	Wide range	April-June	An acid, peaty soil is essential. Shade or semi-shade, ideally in woodland	No regular attention other than mulching with peat if necessary
Ribes sanguineum (flowering currant)	Popular spring-flowering shrub with sprays of pinkish flowers. 'Pulborough Scarlet' is a good red. 'King Edward' a deep crimson	H:2.4m (8ft) S:2.1m (7ft)	March-April	Prefers well-drained soil in light shade or sun	Prune, if necessary, immediately after flowering
Senecio × '**Sunshine**' (syn. *S. greyi*)	A useful grey-foliaged shrub for a small garden. Bushy habit, white-felted leaves, and yellow, daisy-like flowers	H:900mm (3ft) S:900mm (3ft)	July-Aug	Prefers a well-drained soil in sun or light shade	Remove straggly shoots during the summer months
Skimmia japonica	A neat evergreen shrub with small white, fragrant, flowers and red berries	H:1.5m (5ft) S:1.5m (5ft)	April-May	Undemanding, but avoid a limy soil. Grows in shade	No routine work required, but male and female plants are needed for berries
Taxus baccata (yew)	An evergreen conifer, well-known in churchyards. Makes a fine hedge, and is a good topiary plant	H:3m+ (10ft+) S:3m+ (10ft)	–	Tolerant of most soils, including chalk, but avoid a damp site. Will grow in sun or shade	Plant in Oct or April
Viburnum carlesii	A medium-sized shrub with clusters of white flowers, with a sweet, daphne-like fragrance	H:1.5m (5ft) S:1.5m (5ft)	April-May	Likes a moist but well-drained soil, in sun or partial shade	No regular pruning is required, but remove old stems from crowded bushes in winter

INDEX

ACKNOWLEDGEMENTS

The publishers thank the following for providing the photographs in this book: Heather Angel 4, 9 above; Pat Brindley 17, 31; Derek Gould 24 below, 38, 45 left, 47, 54 above right, 58; Susan Griggs agency (Michael Boys) 35; Margaret Mclean 3; Harry Smith Photographic Collection 11 below, 18 above left, 19 below, 23, 26, 29, 32 above, 36, 37 above, 40 above, 44 below, 56 above, 59; Michael Warren/Photos Horticultural 6-7, 10, 14, 15, 27 right, 41, 42, 44 above, 45 below, 48, 49 main picture, 50 above, 51, 53 below, 57; Elizabeth Whiting and Associates 33.

The following photographs were taken specially for Octopus Books: Michael Boys 7 inset, 19 above right, 39 below, 43, 49 below inset, 55 above; Jerry Harpur 9 below, 11 above, 20 above, 39 above, 40 below, 46, 50 below, 52 below, 54 left, 55 below; Neil Holmes 12, 13, 18, 30, 37 below, 56 below; George Wright 21 left, 47 inset, 49 above inset, 52 above, 53 above.

Drawings by Will Giles, Stan North, Liz Pepperell